NOTHING HELD BACK

Truth & Fiction from WriteGirl

Also from WriteGirl Publications:

THREADS, 2002
BOLD INK: Collected Voices of Women and Girls, 2003
PIECES OF ME: The Voices of WriteGirl, 2004

Raves for 2005 Independent Publisher Award Anthology Finalist, *PIECES OF ME:*

"Wow! I couldn't stop reading this. Talk about goosebumps! This book will shock you—
and make you think—and make you FEEL—all at the same time!"
 R.L. Stine

"All the boldness, unselfconsciousness, lack of vanity and beautiful raw talent that is
usually tamped down by adulthood bursts from these pages and announces a formi-
dable new crop of young writers."
 Meghan Daum, Author of *The Quality of Life Report* and *My Misspent Youth*

"*Pieces of Me* is a riveting collection of creative writing produced by girls and women
with enormous talent. On every page you'll encounter fresh voices and vibrant poems
and stories that pull you into these writers' worlds, into the energy of their lives."
 Vendela Vida, Author of *And Now You Can Go* and *Girls on the Verge*

NOTHING HELD BACK

Truth & Fiction from WriteGirl

WriteGirl Publications

Los Angeles

Nothing Held Back: The Voices of WriteGirl

Executive Editor:	Keren Taylor
Editors:	Marna Bunger
	Elena Karina Byrne
	Janine Coughlin
	Leslie Davis
	Allison Deegan
	Karen Girard
	Cecilia Lee
	Jennifer Repo
	Mae Respicio
	Jayna Rust
	Katherine Taylor
Book Design:	Danielle Foushée, *www.daniellefoushee.com*
Photography:	Lisa Beebe, Cecilia Lee, Jessica Young
Printing:	Donahue Printing, Kevin Grandon

FIRST EDITION
Printed in the United States of America

ISBN #: 09741251-2-1

Orders, inquiries and correspondence should be addressed to:

WriteGirl Publications
Los Angeles, California
www.writegirl.org
info@writegirl.org

Thank you to everyone who contributed to this WriteGirl book for your courage and vulnerability in turning your insides out and putting yourself on paper.

I feel very creative
& even wonderful
when I write.
It's like medicine
& it's fun too.

ACKNOWLEDGMENTS

Many people contributed to the production of this book—and I can't thank everyone enough.

I especially want to thank all our authors for their humor, wisdom and courage. Not only are you tremendously talented writers, you're amazing people, too.

We get so many incredible pieces from the girls and women of WriteGirl that our editing job gets harder every year. What a great problem to have, right? Lucky for us, we have an extremely dedicated, talented editorial team: Marna Bunger, Elena Karina Byrne, Janine Coughlin, Leslie Davis, Allison Deegan, Karen Girard, Cecilia Lee, Jennifer Repo, Mae Respicio, Jayna Rust and Katherine Taylor. Thank you for pulling miracles from the teeth of deadlines, expertly untangling words and laughing your way through some marathon editing sessions.

I'd especially like to thank Allison Deegan for her ability to nudge writers up to the plate. Many girls' and womens' voices are here in this book because of her encouragement and tenacious communication.

Cecilia Lee's technical wizardry and attention to detail made just about every aspect of creating this book go more smoothly. Thank you so much for making all those last-minute, late-night quick fixes and for being so generous with your time.

I want to thank Danielle Foushée for the design of this book. Despite being new to the WriteGirl family, Danielle listened patiently and created the perfect look and feel. Because of your inventive choices, Danielle, our words have a place to shine.

I'd like to thank Jacques Taylor for extraordinary patience and support as I navigate through the challenging rapids of producing a book a year. I'm so grateful for your insights and honesty.

And special thanks to Wasabi, our chocolate lab, whose gentle nose reminded us to take much-needed breaks and whose tail-wagging enthusiasm kept everyone smiling.

Keren Taylor

Contents

Everyday Heroes *(Tribute)*

The Thrill of Being *(Self)*

Ha! Ha! Ha!

She Changes *(Transformation)*

Fireflies in My Hand *(Philosophical/Dreamy)*

City of Some Angels *(Los Angeles)*

Soles of Our Shoes *(Traveling)*

In Retrospect *(Reminiscing)*

Writing Experiments

This Is WriteGirl

"Seeing WriteGirl in action was a truly amazing experience — these girls are empowered and finding their voices. What a gift this program is to their lives."
— Geena Davis

WriteGirl supporter Geena Davis, pictured here with high school student Angela Martinez (left) and WriteGirl Executive Director Keren Taylor (right).

INTRODUCTION

There is a great amount of abandon in this book. Writers gave over to their creative minds and abandoned their fear of the white page or their negative inner chatter. All year long, WriteGirl asked girls and women to try new genres of writing, to investigate their past, to explore their identity, to examine their family and culture, to pay tribute to someone they love or someone they had lost. We wrote to music, we wrote on posters with thick black markers, we wrote in each other's journals, we wrote outside in the sun, we wrote for hours at a time and we didn't want to stop because once you break free from whatever stops you from writing, the flow of ideas and creative energy is so strong and so much fun that you don't ever want to put down your pen or let your fingers leave the keyboard.

Throughout the book, you'll find quotes from our WriteGirls—soundbites that we call "threads." They're reflections on writing and life that we write at the end of every WriteGirl workshop or event. These quick snapshots of our members' experiences and perspectives always remind me of the power that can be contained in even a very few well-chosen (or impulsively tossed out) words.

This book is a collection of young emerging writers, seasoned pros and everything in between. So, drop your preconceptions about poetry or stories or essays, or about women or girls or Angelenos and fall into these pages and all the cracks in between. Then, by the time you get to the writing experiments, you'll be ready to face your own white page and abandon anything holding you back.

Keren Taylor

Blame Me

for
Everything

FAMILY

I thought there were no words to describe my family, but now that I've started writing about them, the words keep coming.

Progress is sometimes invisible.

Empowering the creative tends to empower everything.

This poem really has to do with my mother and our relationship over the years. We are so much alike, and I admire her so much. I wanted to describe how I feel about our relationship in as few words as possible. It was difficult to write such a concise poem.

FIREWATER

A textbook example,

a mother shakes a tree and an apple doesn't fall far.

She eats the fruit of the same girl in the backseat of that car.

Canned oranges, dripping, wet

cotton T-shirts like summer,

like starfruit holidays in chlorine and whiskey—

no ocean water surprises,

sea sand, salt,

like mother like daughter.

I wrote this about a lunch with my mother.

LUNCH AT THE HEIGHTS

I was seated in a corner trying to read a Grisham novel and drinking iced tea. The restaurant, normally filled with professors and out-of-town guests, was filled with groups of three and four ladies dining on the sumptuous meals, chatting loudly and ordering individual desserts. I was relieved when my mother walked in because it was far too loud to read.

"I got the time of my appointment wrong," my mother said. "I had to reschedule."

My mother has short white hair that curls softly around her face. She's old lady round, but not obese; after all, she's sixty-seven. She's five-foot-six and wears no make-up except for a mauve lipstick that comes off when she eats. She was cheerful despite a day of small disappointments. In addition to her missed hair appointment we had an unsuccessful quest for some children's art supplies and only mild success getting curtain rod end pieces. However, she saw taking me out to eat as an accomplishment and in a way it was. My last boyfriend, Steven, used to take me out for elegant meals, and I needed to replace the memories. I needed to connect delicious food with someone other than him. She ordered the seafood cake and I had cod with eggplant and parsnips.

"I think when you go back to Los Angeles you should start attending church." This had become a favorite topic. What she meant was I could meet a virtuous, social-minded man if I attended church. "Church is not religious," she said with no intended sarcasm. "It's a social institution."

"The kind of man I want doesn't go to church."

She stared at me in frustration with a new look that she had only recently acquired. Soft and filled with worry, it lacked the fierce determination that had filled most of her looks in the thirty some years that I had known her. It was vulnerable and more than a little sad.

"You're not going to solve my life, Mom. No matter how often you juggle the variables of what you consider my options, you are never going to solve my life."

"I suppose that's true," she said in a rare moment of rationality. We focused the conversation on how scrumptious the food was and afterwards ordered two desserts.

I wrote this poem last summer when I visited my sister in Los Osos and found a small empty bird's nest laying on the ground. Writing it helped me let go of my adult daughters.

BLUE WOMAN FINDS AN EMPTY NEST

Hiking along the western ridge
step by breath by step by breath
keeping her own time,
Blue Woman crossed the bridge of letting go
and found an empty nest.

She picked it up; it fitted in her palm.
Soft with hair, dead grasses, cotton bits,
deftly constructed, perfectly round
a small weedy bowl bereft of egg and chick:
a psalm of emptiness.

In the distance a volcano plumed,
the great eagle's head emerging
fire flaming into wings.
Blue Woman's face in the red light
purpled with fear.

Where are they? Are they safe?
Are they happy? Are they sad?
Did I lose them? Did I forget to write?
Was it something I did or said?

She fought the mother panic, talking to herself,
tempted to trade faith for fear:
to live their lives so she wouldn't have to
live her own.

Blue Woman had reached the top.
Behind her the bridge was burning.
Leaning over, she looked in the mountain's mouth,
perfectly round, hotly aswirl
with fibrous fires of copper and gold,
and tossed the nest.
It flew up, heat-borne,
spinning bright embers out of itself,

This is an excerpt from my memoir.

GROWING UP ANGLO

I am twelve years old and Kathleen, my sister, is ten. We are told our mother, who is fifty-three, is close to death. She is no longer just sick, the doctor is sure "she could go anytime."

My sister and I are allowed into the dim hospital room with its sharp unpleasant smell. My cadaverous, bald mother lies sideways on white sheets. Bleeding tumors circumference her neck. Extensive bandages to stop the blood flow make her look like she's the victim of whiplash. I kiss her soft withered cheek. With effort, she opens her beautiful hazel eyes and her gaze drifts from Kathleen to me. My mother smiles at both of us with her pale lips. She clenches a tiny blue piece of paper in her right hand and I take it from her.

Her penmanship is something I always admired and imitated. She got angry at me once for taking a fountain pen and tracing over her signature on a school form that I was to hand in to my second grade teacher. But I could not resist seeing what it felt like to move up and down with the curves of her signature. When I moved with the letters, it was almost like I was her.

Staring at the paper, her perfect penmanship, destroyed like everything else, is now a cluster of wavy lines and curls that must be deciphered. "Be good," I read. A nurse tells us we must leave the room and wait down the hallway. I place the paper on the metal dresser. Later, much later, years later, I wondered what happened to that fragment of her.

My father guides us into the hallway. Kathleen and I hold him around his ample waist. With downward gaze, we march in solemn sequence, right left, right left, the square black and white hospital tiles passing underneath our three pairs of shoes. We sit and wait for her to die. My father slumps over in a brown leather chair. His head held in his hands with his eyes hidden from us. Kathleen sits next to me on a long couch. Across the room, there is a painting of the archangel Gabriel, his wings outstretched, protectively hovering over three women and two men in white robes.

"Daddy," I murmur, "Mommy is going straight to heaven, isn't she?" I give him these words in part to remind him that she is going to a better place but more for reassurance that there is such a place of ascendance.

His head jerks up and his blue eyes are red around the rims. With his nicotine-stained fingers, he has made track marks in his white thick hair from his grasping and ungrasping. He hits me with his angry tone. "Of course she is." My father turns away from me and I hear his faint sobs above the hum of the fluorescent lights. I dissolve into my seat. Stunned by his anger and scared by his sadness, I glare back at Gabriel. My mother died the following morning.

I wrote this in the Creative Nonfiction Workshop. Up to that point, I'd never spoken of my feelings about this day. Writing this was very cathartic for me.

ROOFTOP PERSPECTIVE

The party was fun enough. Laughing people with cocktails in hand; the view of downtown Chicago and the lake from this rooftop, stunning on a clear June day. I tried hard to fit in with the jovial mood. Staring down at the freshly barbequed chicken on my plate I wondered why I even put it there. All I could hear was my mother's voice, "It's a sin to waste God's food." In spite of her perch on my shoulder, I set the plate down in hopes of someone else adopting it. Cigarette smoke danced lazily around my head in the stillness of the humid day. I walked alone to the edge of the building and inhaled the meandering beauty of the lakefront. How many years had I walked that path raising money for MS, enjoying the social time it allowed Kelli and me? A refreshing scene from our neighborhood in the suburbs. All those years of not knowing anyone with MS, but doing the walks regardless. My duty. My fun. How ironic that the news today would change all that. That today I would learn that my brother was diagnosed with the disease, and that somehow it was my fault.

Stephanie Almendarez, age 17

This is how my parents, my eight-year-old sister and my two-year-old brother looked to me through my five-year-old eyes.

PICTURE PERFECT

Papi is tall and I always want him to carry me. Like when the earthquake came, in the night, he had to carry me and Jonci. But Gilma just kept sleeping.

Mami has soft brown hair. Her hands are so smooth. She touches my eyes and I could fall asleep.

Gilma is a baronila. She dresses and acts like a boy. While the boy across the street, Giovanni, and me play hide and seek, Gilma and Giovanni's cousin, Juan, play baseball.

Jonci is always drinking milk. Sometimes I steal his bottle. Especially when it's chocolate. My mom hits me on the hands. I get mad. I cry sometimes, too.

I am coqueta. I pull down my sleeves to show my shoulders. For Halloween, I dressed up as a bride. Juan dressed up as a groom. But I want to marry Giovanni.

Cecilia Hae-Jin Lee, mentor

I wrote this poem, which was originally published in the Asian Pacific American Journal, before I became a food writer and later discovered that much of my writing was about eating. I was peeling a tangerine and thinking about my older sister. We are still very close and love to share food together.

TANGERINE SHARING

"The smallest ones are the best," my sister
would say to me, lying
and I knew it in my five-year-old heart
even as I extended my hand to accept
that pock-marked orb

We sat there on that house floor
with the bag between us
our barefoot toes curled
against the coldness of the wood

We made tangerine boats
that afternoon—curved half moons
gathering our slippery seeds, hoping
for the sweet squirting surprises, hoping
to hide our stained jeans where
our oily hands had wiped
one too many times. Our legs wet,
our bellies satisfied

My sister,
she held that bag by her side, hoarding
those fruits as if they were golden treasures
to be hidden deep, hidden long, hidden forever
until our fingernails were filled
with its spongy secrets
long before our nails grew
long and manicured

Pass me another one, sister,
and we will share the long ago afternoons
of little girls, before the sun sets
on our tangerine boats.

Deborah Bramwell, age 15

Originally, I wrote this in proper, formal language. The going was slow and tedious, and the story not terribly engrossing. One night I tried writing it in a more vernacular style, and found the road far smoother. I stayed up until 3 a.m. and wrote nearly twenty thousand words.

ROBINS AT MIDNIGHT

Since bein' taken away I'd not thought of Ma, not really, which I guess made it a whole lot easier, because suddenly I did think of her and me bein' dead and her not knowin,' and how it would just break her heart what was probably nearly broke already, me havin' disappeared like, even if Will went to her which he better've or I'll pound him real good, and suddenly I realize all this is bein' said out loud though real quiet, my feelings and worries all spillin' out of me and tears with them. And then Ma … I got it, all of a sudden then, why Ma was so always angry when I slept with the spiders under the floor and did stupid things like that, not like pickin' apples maybe but like when I broke my arm, it's because she cares about me and she hates me bein' hurt and that's it, and oh how I wish I could tell her that, just so's she'd know how I understand and that I love her, and what's gonna happen to me and …

Suddenly I go real quiet, just snivelin' little sobs escapin' my throat, because David's done somethin' really brave and puts his arms around me, and now he's holdin' me against his chest which goes to show he must've been a real nice da just like Will's. When he's sort of cradlin' me I'm no longer afraid for what's goin' to happen to me, just sort of content and comfortable. My tears stop wantin' to come but I make them keep on comin,' because I don't want David to let me go, not yet. I'm not ready for the world—quite.

Jennifer Carcamo, age 15

I was inspired to write this poem during a WriteGirl workshop. We were asked to write about an object. When I first saw this pot, I couldn't think of anyone else but my two grandmothers (abuelitas)! This poem brought back wonderful memories.

MEMORIA DE MI ABUELITAS

Abuelita Amparo has a little ceramic pot
With curvaceous flowers of
Blue and white
The colors of our country.

On her bureau
Where she keeps her most precious jewels,
Next to the cross of Jesus Christ.

My Abuelita Amparo asked me to fetch her earrings
He raced to the pot
To prove he was worthy
To get them first.

He snapped the lid so hard and fast
That the fragile material
Chipped!

I peeked over the pot
Suddenly
Overwhelmed by
Aromas of oatmeal and dry perfumed roses:
The smell of my Abuelita Clarita.

I picked up the lid
Along with four other
Pieces of chipped ceramic
Colors of blue and white

Firm.
Familiar.
Memorable.
Just like the hands of my dear Abuelita Clarita.

MY GRANDMOTHER'S SECRET

I was home alone one night when I heard the chain on the front gate clinking like someone was trying to get in. I was imagining the headline in the next day's newspaper, "Girl, Home Alone, Dies by Stabbing." But it was a false alarm. When I peered out the front window, a woman dressed in sweats stood in front of my house. She told me that she was my father's cousin, the daughter of my father's sister from my grandmother's first marriage.

My grandmother's first marriage? No one knew she had been married before.

My grandmother Lily lived in Gilroy, a farming town just an hour from San Jose, Calif. She met and married a man named Antonio. Together, they had twelve children. Around 1953, she left Antonio and their children because he was an abusive alcoholic. I couldn't imagine my grandmother having twelve children and then leaving them behind. She was a woman with a lot of strength and tenderness.

I called her Grandma White because she had white hair, though her skin was dark, to distinguish her from my maternal grandmother, who had brown hair.

In the mornings, I usually found Grandma White outside, dressed in her straw hat and black Keds, pulling weeds and talking to her roses and snapdragons. She grew aloe vera in her backyard. I remember my grandmother rubbing that aloe vera on the rash on my arms.

Whenever I stayed at her house, Grandma White made salad, arranging the apples, iceberg lettuce and grapes into a big, fruity sunflower with cottage cheese in the middle. When she scrambled eggs she loved to show off by flipping them in the air. She cooked me red snapper, brought to her by a woman who lived two doors down. I loved sucking the salty meat off its little splintery bones. We'd have tea parties with tea brewed from the mint leaves that grew right outside her kitchen, and we used her fine china that she never let anyone else touch.

In the evenings, she would cook arroz con pollo or a boiling pot of menudo, and then we watched sitcoms like "Sister, Sister" or her old black and white Dolores Del Rio movies on the Spanish channel. Unlike my mother, she never watched those telenovelas starring Laura Leon. Grandma always pointed out the actors who were "in heaven."

She kept a lot of paper that I used for drawing. I liked to draw Marilyn Monroe and monsters, which she would proudly display on her sliding closet doors.

Grandma White always told me how strong and helpful I was because I helped her bake carrot cake and clean the house. When I came home crying because the children at my elementary school were making fun of me, she told me the next time I see them,

I should just tell them to go to hell. She never doubted my superhero strength, even though I was a little girl.

Although we were close, I sometimes did cause a little mischief. My grandmother had a collection of flamboyant muu muus that she wore around the house. One day, I snuck into her room with a pair of scissors and shredded a cherry red muu muu into strips. Since it wasn't anything fancy, she wasn't angry, but when she bought a purple Easter dress, she told me she bought it so I could cut it up. But I didn't.

It saddens me that her children from her first marriage do not have memories like I have. These small things show how special a woman she was and how much they and she must have lost when she left.

At twenty-two I discovered that I had been adopted and raised by my maternal grand-parents. I believed that they were my biological parents, but one of my sisters was actually my birth mother. My natural father, whom I never met, had been murdered when I was ten. It wasn't until I entered my forties that I was finally ready to begin sifting through my childhood and piecing together the bigger picture of my life.

OUR LADY OF GRACE

I have a memory of the moment my soul crash-landed into my body, somewhere in the middle of the last century, in a time caught between conformity and rebellion. The territory was foreign, the language familiar. Maybe it was spring. Perhaps it was fall. Definitely not summer or winter. No snow, not enough heat.

The sun was a brilliant, pulsing, golden orb set against the backdrop of a beautiful sky-blue sky. Can sky be any other shade of blue? I knew about blue and its many varieties. Wasn't yet aware that it was more than just a color. Didn't know that one could sing the blues or play the blues or just be blue. You could drink Blue Nun or be a blue nun. Krishna was a blue god and one day there would be a blue meanie and a blue smurf. Everyone can see that they are blue. You just take one look at them and you know. Some people don't appear to be blue but they feel blue. They may speak in blue tones, but not the blue tones of a comic like Redd Fox.

On that day long ago, blue was just the color of clear sky in daylight. I was on a street in a city. Not downtown, pressed between ominous skyscrapers and serious suited businessmen rushing from important meeting to important meeting. Not in the suburbs, that carefree land of private lawns and smiling aproned homemakers baking cakes and burping babies.

This place is somewhere in between, an urban buffer zone where downtown meets suburb. Families stacked on top of and next to each other, in row after row, square after square, of duplexes. Family-friendly barracks known as courts, where judgments are met-ed out daily during the trials of these lives of quiet aspiration. In the center of each court, an open green patch of lawn to be shared by all. This is a world where sometimes moms work and sometimes dads don't. Children can have children for parents and parents can have parents for children. Nothing is as it appears and appearances are everything. Truth may be fiction and fiction may stand-in for truth. Paradise on a blue-collar budget.

Kristin Petersen, mentor

This came from the guided writing experiment in the Poetry Workshop. We were given a specific direction for each line of the poem, like "use a visual image" or "write a phrase that uses alliteration." This was the first guided poetry writing I'd ever done. At first, I was a little skeptical that much would come out of it, but I was surprised and pleased with the outcome.

RELATIVITY

She needs this.

For now, for her, I will condescend.

In the end, I will be a pirate.

I will be water, swallowing her.

I can eat this child.

I can save her if I'm clever.

She needs this.

They call me tin-tin, leave me flowers.

I give them cherry blossom kisses

and smooth them into silk.

I am a cupboard to collect and keep them.

I will be stone; they will rest on me.

My tangled heart adopts their knots, unravels them.

I steal their hearts to the sea, but I leave my pieces behind.

Alix K. Pham, mentor

I wrote this story for my father, who loves gardening. When I tried seeing him through the plants' eyes, I came to understand him better.

THE GARDENER'S TALE

They watched him silently: a solitary figure of a man, worn down by life and its trials, nearly killed by a machete during the war. He stood caved-in at times, bent as if from a heavy, invisible burden that perched on his shoulders, causing him pain and sorrow, making his height even shorter than five feet, five inches. His once lustrous black hair was now streaked with heavy silver and laid like a mantle of fresh snow parted on the left side and brushed back to reveal a broad forehead, a stamp of deep thought. His eyes were a dark brown, sunken into the sockets as if a lifetime of sight had been too much. They had no wish to see more. His ears too had closed themselves off to the world outside by pressing themselves closely to his head. He had a broad, broken nose that was no longer sensitive to smell except to the fragrance of the garden. A swarthy complexion, compact body, large hands and callous-hewed feet completed the Gardener's frame. He was once a strong man; at least that was how the older plants remembered him to be. The young only saw what he was now—weary. He was weary from obligations that never seemed to disappear or allow him a moment's respite. The man needed shelter from the world outside, from his stained family and from the ghosts of his past inside. So he came here to be with the plants. They were his friends and companions, the children born solely of his sweat and labor. They were a part of him, spanning generations of noble bloodlines, unbroken and pure. They stood, proud to be his inner family and friends, these children of nature.

The thorny bushes of roses were bright as the blood shed on battlefields of his native country. Purplish-black irises stood tall and unyielding against adversity. Laughing and dancing pansies and lilies of the valley swayed with memories of friends, family and a past forever gone. Young Japanese pear-apple trees stood with their branches heavily laden with the promises of succulent fruits of rich life.

The wind gently blew their leaves and the rustling sound was like the chiming of tiny bells singing soft songs. It was only here that he was truly home. A sanctuary from the coldness of the outside world, a place he belonged... unconditionally.

Marietta Putignano, mentor

I began writing this as I sat with my dad as he grew weaker and weaker. Four days later, I held his hand as I watched him take his last breath.

FORTRESS

If only I could take away your pain
as I watch you struggle
oxygen, painkillers, pumps
The disease courses through you like a thief
stealing your strength, but not your will
Your delicate skin aches with every touch
gentle eyes heavy with medicated slumber
The amber desert shines outside your window,
pink hyacinth blooms abundantly,
unknowingly
We gather together as much for you as for each other
surrounding you like a fortress
your spirit fights as you drift out to sea
only to float back to the safety of the shore
every smile a gift, every wink a priceless treasure
The stillness comes, the promise of peace
your soul soaring, singing the aria of your life
If only I could wake you
with my love

Deborah Bramwell, age 15

In ninth grade, my English class focused heavily on Greek mythology. I sapped every droplet of information I could, and this is the love child of that knowledge and a very long stint on an airplane.

THE KING OF THE GODS

Her father had seated himself on the couch. He watched her over a steeple of fingers. Hermes, leaning against the wall, observed one, then the other.

"My name is Zeus, King of the Gods."

For a moment there was silence. Then Helen's shoulders began to shake, and she doubled over in silent laughter. The first sound to tear from her lips rang like a sob. Indeed, fat tears rolled down her cheeks when she ceased her laughing and gasped for breath like a fish out of water. "No," she said at last, "seriously. Who are you?"

"I am Zeus, King of the Gods," said Zeus.

Helen extended the usual challenge: "Prove it."

Zeus, enraged, sputtered, "Prove it? Prove it! Let me tell you, in the old days, no one would dare challenge me. Men would be grateful, honored to be my sons! No one challenged me!"

The roar of this last sentence resonated through the room in a physical echo. The young man in the second armchair said, "Why don't you just show her how powerful you are, Dad?"

"I will!"

He pointed one finger at a magazine on the short table before them; it burst into flames and very shortly burned out. When the fire was gone, no trace remained of it: no singe marks, no ashes. Zeus smiled, pleased with himself. Helen yawned. "Modern pyrotechnics bore me," she said, "on such tiny scales."

Zeus's face turned a furious red, then purple, amusing Helen greatly. When he suddenly stood, towering so that his shoulders stooped to avoid hitting the ceiling, where suddenly a thunderstorm replaced white stucco, Helen was more impressed. "Do not question the King of the Gods!" His words roared like hurricanes in her ears and tore through her body like fire. Satisfied, Zeus shrank back to a more human form. He spoke, but Helen could not hear. She was holding her ears, where blisters blossomed, and shuddering.

"Boss?" Hermes was still reclining against the wall. "I think she is going to—"

He did not need to finish. Helen bent her head over the carpet and retched. The messenger had expected this, not by any uncanny power of foresight, but because any driver knows the signs of approaching illness.

Even Zeus felt sorry then, seeing the poor state of his child. Angry blisters bubbled in her ears, and small patches of blood were appearing where his voice had torn through her skin. He looked at the girl, shocked, then pulled out a sleek cellular telephone and punched a few digits. "Athena? I need you and the twins here, five minutes ago!"

Hermes rolled his eyes as Zeus snapped the cell phone shut. Why the King of the Gods repeated every silly thing he heard in a Hollywood film was beyond Hermes. As he told Jesus on their drinking nights, he was just the messenger. Like any postal worker, it would cost his job to interfere with the gods.

Ariana Horwitz, age 14

STROLLING

Father, do you remember our strolls by the beach?

My small hand holding your strong one

The sea breeze winding its grip around our senses

Seagulls squawking as we went by

Our bare feet sinking into the warm sand

Crabs and dolphins playing like children

Do you remember our strolls on the beach, father?

I do, just like I remember you leaving mom and me

After my parents' divorce, my Armenian grandmother systematically went through all the family photos and cut my mother out of each picture. I wrote this as an adult, looking back on the absurdity of my family's behavior, and learned to find humor in tragedy.

FAMILY LEGACY

"Hard life, this. I move far, far away from my village,
so young, so fresh..." Suddenly, I'm visible.
"You a pretty girl. What's your name?
Ah, yes, you are my son's youngest. C'mere, let me see you."
She smells of lemon juice, chopped garlic,
patting a lap I fear I'll die in one of these days.

Upstairs, a chair rasps across a floor.
Her eyes, hard black olive pits, flicker upward—
they have hated one another for five decades,
but never said it out loud. No one in this family
uses words with weight to them.

Queena and Pete shuffle around each other
all day, an old person's dance. "Mama..."
he shouts, "Mama...," then mutters something in Armenian.
She whispers, "He tries to get me put away, you know?
I collect glass horses, see?" Queena points to a display case
she allows no one to touch.

"He thinks I think they're alive."
The old woman jerks a crooked thumb over her shoulder,
nodding conspiratorially to me.

They keep a diapered monkey named Baby in the laundry room—
swinging amongst the pipes, it throws the contents of its diapers
at me as if to say, "I'm number one here, not you."
Children have no place here, not expensive ones, like me.

I'm allergic to the cheese pastries Queena makes
each winter of my visits. I tell her, but she doesn't believe me.
She says I willed the rash behind my knees to spite her.
Baby nestles in her scary lap, sucking its thumb while
outside snow entombs the house, our primitive life.

Katherine Taylor, mentor

Sometimes, in little family squabbles, irremediable misunderstandings and massive communication breakdowns take place. This story is from a collection to be published by HarperCollins in spring 2006.

THE ROUTINE

My brother and my mother are having an argument about politics. My brother slams the newspaper onto the table and stomps upstairs to his room, as if he were a child. It's a big house with a long staircase. He continues shouting as he marches up and out of earshot. "You!" he shouts. "You!"

"Why do you do that?" I say to her.

"What did I do?"

"You!" he shouts. "Are insane!"

"Why don't you just agree with him?"

"I don't agree with him."

"Why don't you just pretend?"

"Because I will not lie to my children." She brushes dirt from button mushrooms. She tosses one after the other into a large bowl. She does not look up, she gently rubs each mushroom with a cloth. I can see the bald spot on the top of her head.

"Then don't lie. Change your mind." One moment we were three polite people sitting peacefully in my parents' kitchen, cleaning mushrooms and reading the paper. The next moment my brother and mother were violent, shouting, crazy-eyed people.

My mother's political views sometimes have little logic. Often during political arguments with my mother, her retorts include "Because it offends me!" or "That's just the way it is." Unfortunately, the only argument to be made with my mother is usually, "You're nuts," which she does not try to defend.

"He brought it up," she says.

"He didn't bring it up, he was reading the paper."

She is visibly pained. There is that line she gets down the center of her forehead, the same line you see in her wedding photos. In a moment she will open the refrigerator and eat every leftover she finds. She is not visibly pained to have disagreed with my brother, she is visibly pained at the thought of his being a son with ideas that offend her.

"I don't care. I think what I think."

"You ought to think about changing your mind."

"He's wrong."

"I think you're wrong." I am relieved the argument has been so brief and that so far no one has put a fist through the sliding glass door.

"I know what you think," she says. She stops a moment. She says, "I am his mother."

I pick up the newspaper where Ethan has left it.

There is a long silence. She opens the refrigerator and takes the lemon sole I brought home from dinner last night. "So," she says, opening the box, eating the sole, "What else?"

When I wrote this, I had to acknowledge that religion played a bigger role in my life than I thought.

MIRACLE OF THE EGGS

The first miracle I ever witnessed was watching Lola, my Filipina grandmother, conjure up two desserts from just one carton of eggs. For Catholic kids raised on stories about the loaves and fishes and water turning into wine, we were primed to believe in kitchen magic.

It was a ritual. The minute we saw Lola take the carton out of the fridge, we gathered in the kitchen. Like altar boys we assembled the sacred tools: glass bowls, electric mixer with its pair of steel beaters, measuring cups and spoons, sifter with old sheets of wax paper folded inside, tube pan.

She would order my sister and me to wash and dry bowl and beaters completely, warning us that one speck of grease or water would defile everything. She'd measure out a small amount of cake flour and sugar and tell our little brother to sift them separately. Being the youngest, he'd make a mess of it and be sent away from the table with a wave of her arthritic hand. By then the bowls and beaters were ready, and she'd start separating the eggs. Those bony, withered fingers turned suddenly graceful as she cracked each egg, holding it high and letting the clear egg white ooze into a puddle in the bowl. She dropped the yolks into another bowl and stacked the shells into a pile. When she tossed in the teaspoon of vanilla and a pinch of cream of tarter, we were already plugging in the mixer and positioning ourselves around the table for the transformation.

The clear ooze turned to a white cloud as the beaters went around and around the bowl. Lola would signal, and we'd take turns sprinkling in the sugar one tablespoon at a time. The three of us would lose track of whose turn it was with the spoon and a spat would erupt. Lola would shush us, grab the spoon and finish the job herself. Silent and pouting, we'd stand back from the table. My sister would be summoned to help fold the cake flour into the high, fluffy cloud. My brother would be forgiven and awarded the job of slowly turning the tube pan while Lola gently pushed the silky, white mound inside. When she stepped away to put the cake into the oven, we three would descend on the beaters, bowl and spatula to lick away the sweet batter. When Lola turned back to the table, she would discover a mess and three sticky miscreants. With one gruff shout she would banish us to the garden. There we would weed, reflect and scatter the crushed eggshells at the base of her anointed plants.

On our return, the angel food cake would be cooling upside down in the tube pan. Next to it there would be two golden leche flans glistening with caramel syrup. We had taken part in the ritual that begat the cake. The flan would remain a divine mystery that required our belief.

The hungry do not question a miracle.

My mentee, Lena, and I were sitting in a coffee shop in Pasadena, and one of us came up with the topic of bees. I don't remember if it was her idea or mine, but we sat and wrote for ten minutes in our journals. Later, I came back to this and worked it into a poem.

ONE SWALLOW

Does not make a summer, nor one bee a flower; but it
Can't be managed without her, either. Vanilla beans
Wait in the wings with orange and other fruit trees for
Pollinators, rainwater, the birds that eat pits and seeds,
Butterflies that suck nectar. A tiny farm each flower,
Its migrant workers smarter than all of us, more tenacious.
Long ago, in the dark ages, learned men studied alchemy,
A dead end, a drone, the cuckoo of chemistry. One gold
Bird is not spring, but a bee can bring the first hot sting
Of summer. Just last week at the end of our street a house
Was blocked off with big, yellow signs: Warning: Bees.
Two days later in our house ants came up like crumbs
Of reddish-brown lava flowing though cabinets and our
Dirty laundry, looping through the dog's bowl, crawling
Along the defunct cables in all four closets. Will they
Find the baby? Will I lose her bit by bit or in a swarm?
Should I look for boric acid? Powdered flowers? That
Is also magic, the insecticides, cans of anti-bee spray and
Sticky traps. I know that without flowers there would be
No creatures, no sex, no husband and wife, no infant in
Her white crib, lips wet with breakfast milk, eyelids like
Moth wings, new mother hovering, pressing sugar ants
Between thumb and finger.

Feelings of

of

RELATIONSHIPS

Peculiar Intensity

There are girls out there like me.

Everything works out in the end.

I'm not the only one who's had a broken heart.
I will survive!

Simple things make me the happiest. I feel so happy when I read this poem. It makes the world make sense.

PATIENT VOCABULARY

Oh, boy with taco and many packets of hot sauce

I spoke in a bad accent inches

from you and not knowing you were there.

Turning to see and waiting

for the world to fall out of the windows for you.

Sphinx in your

hand tomorrow. Bird

in your hand tomorrow and in the tree

like an arched back. Even your eyelid

says yes to me.

Columns of your loveliness and quietness

and words that you have chosen

so softly so like cells touching.

Where did you begin, where did you begin

and who knew you then? Where are my bullets?

Where is my gun? Where is my license for the firearms

of love? This is a radical movement to stand

behind you and look at your

neck and your face like an oral history of dogs.

This was inspired by my friend's teen daughter, who chatted with me on the phone one Sunday as if I was one of her girlfriends.

ONE OF THE (TEEN) GIRLS

My friend's fifteen-year-old daughter recently told me on the phone, "Oh my God, my mother is insane, you have to do something." I bit the inside of my cheek, tried to hold back the laughs until I spurted out, "Oh, honey, get used to it. You've got about another forty years before relief is in sight."

Then I realized Kaylene saw me as some sort of responsible adult figure that could reason with her mother—her mother who is just as crazy as me. That made me laugh harder. I mean, Kaylene could be my child if birth control had failed me in my twenties. Instead, she's treating me as her peer. Her mother craves to be her friend. It appears I already am.

Kaylene proceeded to explain that her mother wants her and her two younger brothers to go on a "stupid family hike." She doesn't want to go. She wants to go to the mall to see some friends.

"And will there be boys at the mall?" I asked. She explained that a guy she likes is going to be there.

"Wow. That's cool. I just went to this outdoor mall yesterday on a date with a guy. We had fun," I explained.

I called back a few hours later and told Kaylene's mother my good mall date story. She let Kaylene go to the mall and I was invited to the sweet sixteen party.

Forced family activities are a dime a dozen. Meeting a good guy at the mall is priceless.

Taylor Gray, age 15

When I wrote this, I learned that I don't have to use pronouns so much!

FALLING IN LOVE WITH LOVE

Hands in pocket hugs
with lipgloss starting to wear away
as the "tickle me pink"
on my lips leaves an imprint on his.
Hands clenched together around his
neck pull him closer in
my tiptoe stance almost
a ballerina form.
Never have I seen eyes so close up before.
Dark brown, soft and subtle,
as they peer down at me
as if looking for some answer to an unspoken question.
I knew I was falling in love with love
when I heard his fast-beating heart
reassure me he felt the same.

Lily Mendoza, age 16

Writing poems has become a new outlet for me.

FALLING

Everything was falling apart
My days were always full of anger
But now that I'm with you
My days are full, happy
I still have moments when I feel down
But you're always there trying to make my day

You cherish me, I cherish you
When you kiss me, I feel like I'm being lifted off my feet
When I'm with you, I forget my problems
When you hug me, I feel like never letting you go

When the time comes for us to go to our own homes
I feel like staying with you forever
When we are apart all I can think of is you
Even when I try to work,
You're still in the back of my head
I felt like it was going to be whatever
But it has turned into a long whatever

What would I have been without you?
What would I be doing if I hadn't met you?
All I know is that I'm with you now
And I don't want you to ever leave my side

Karen Girard, mentor

I like to take a little while just to watch people, especially when I feel rushed. In a busy restaurant, I saw a small boy with his arm in a cast tip over his drink. His father cleaned up the mess and, as he helped his son eat, their hands became so synchronized that they seemed like one person.

LANGUAGE OF HANDS

The circumference
Of a small café table
Becomes a universe
When four hands dance
In silent conversation
Reaching across words
To shape the edges
Of understanding
Twist of wrist enclosing
Curve of fingers grasping
Plane of palms upholding
Clarity like a new prayer
Intricate, agile,
Fragile, graceful
The sum of all possibilities
Weaves into happiness.

My friend Barbara and I have been friends most of our lives. In this piece, I celebrate her sabbatical from her life and career.

MIDLIFE CRISIS

Months ago, my friend Barbara cheerfully informed her husband that she was having a midlife crisis, took a sabbatical from her associate professor position and left home to follow U2 around the country. I drove down to spend the night with her in a San Diego Holiday Inn across from the Sports Arena. Barbara and I have been friends since we were twelve. We have survived adolescence, appalling behavior, discomforting fashions and evil lovers. Nothing fazes us about the other. At lunch on the bay, squinting at sailboats, we decided that mid life was the best thing that ever happened to us. Our teens and twenties were pure chaos, a blur. The thirties were still unsettled, but at forty, we washed our faces and relaxed. Farther from youth and closer to death, Barbara has given herself permission to become a fanatic for the summer. This was not a reckless pronouncement, but a joyful determination. She's seeing thirteen U2 shows in eight cities. She's enthusiastically dragging herself to cold, dark parking lots before dawn to set up a lawn chair and wait in line for sixteen hours so she can be one of two hundred people who may, if blessed, feel the spray of Bono's sweat. She does it because she loves the band, she has for twenty-five years, and because she's never had the freedom or the money to chase the thrill of a perfect experience.

We discussed titanic questions over seafood salads: What is consciousness? How do cells, which are inside bodies, inside ecosystems, inside galaxies, all manage to work? Even if it's all an accident, it's inspired. So, here we are, capable of thought, of connection, of being moved. Why not follow a band around the country?

She's made friends with other obsessed fans in ticket lines. They bring each other water and sandwiches, trade pictures of last night's show, share lore about Bono's kindness and are kind to one another in turn. After hours of braving the sun or rain, when the band launches into a song, the fans disclose themselves to each other with a look. They have a collective moment. It's different than making dinner or being stuck in traffic. It's the upside of existence. Last night Barbara called from the line. Bono stopped in his SUV and Barbara blurted something about becoming an anthropologist, partly because of his message. She said she had two students working in Africa and it would mean something to them to have a picture of the two of them. His handlers said, "No time," but Bono stepped out and summoned Barbara across the security tape. He said, "One for my anthropologist friend." He told her that she did important work and put his arm around her. The photograph reveals a diminutive rock star with my friend Barbara, who after nine hours in line looks disheveled and sunburned and electric. She is having the time of her life, and so is Bono, which is the point. And both of them are middle-aged.

Keren Taylor, mentor

I was sitting in a midtown restaurant in Manhattan on a Monday night. There was this woman. And then there was this poem. You never know when a poem will come to you. WriteGirl is all about being in the moment. I was lucky that in the moment I had a napkin and a pen.

TUESDAY, HONEY, CAN WAIT

There's an underbelly to Manhattan on Monday nights.
Candles dance
Coltrane rules
Chateau Margaux Bordeaux pulses through tight lips
and unclenched jaws.
Deals will close by the third glass.
6 p.m. Monday
the day's work is only just beginning,
and if you take things real slow
the room tilts
in your direction
whispers your name,
proclaiming you Queen of New York
moving and snaking
gripping and grinning
and laughing with your head thrown back.
This isn't a power dinner.
This is the world morphing to the magnet of my will
responding to the heavy stock of my business card
the height of my skirt
the elongated shape of my coral fingernails
long lush lashes and bullet-blue lids
my perfectly positioned place in the room
Feng Shui-ing my back to the north wall,
taking Manhattan
one man at a time
starting with Monday.

Nadine Levyfield, age 15

You can take something that really happened to you and add fictional details to make it unique and interesting. (I did see an exotic woman with my teacher at the movies, but I made up everything else!)

WALKING INTO SCHOOL MONDAY MORNING

Walking into school Monday morning, pissed off because I didn't want to be back, I passed by Mr. Ponchak's room. Then I smiled, remembering how I had seen him yesterday at the movies with my friends. The movie theater was about a half hour away from Eagle Rock, where he and I both live. For a person who loved to talk about spending time in Eagle Rock, it seemed strange to see him there, so far away. How surprising it was to see my awkward computer teacher (who reminded me of a smart but socially inept kid getting knocked down by bullies) on the arm of a self-assured, exotic woman with beautiful dark hair. Then I saw he was wearing sunglasses he must have thought were cool, but weren't and reminded me of The Matrix. He was walking with a John Wayne strut, like he owned the place. The combination of seeing this nerdy guy out of the classroom (on the arm of a gorgeous girl), wearing ridiculous sunglasses and walking like that just cracked me up. Laughing hard, I explained to my friends who he was. More, I wondered who she was: a distant relative, or a paid companion? Just then, he gently pushed a piece of her dark hair away from her face and she smiled. Remembering all this, I realize I've been staring at my locker, not even trying to open it. The bell rings, and I head to his class for first period. On his desk, I see a picture of Mr. Ponchak and a woman embracing that I've never noticed before. She's blonde.

I started working on this song on my own time and then finished it with my mentor during one of our weekly sessions.

Kyrsten's mentor, Amy Morton: *"Kyrsten blew me away when she sang the first two verses of this song to me right in the middle of Starbucks. She had the whole melody already laid out in her head. It was a lot of fun to fine-tune the chorus and complete the final verse with her."*

Kyrsten Sprewell, age 13

ANOTHER GURL

I never thought you would be calling me, it's been a while you see.
I never thought we would hook up, after all that stuff.
And I never thought that it would last, cause at first it was so half-assed.

CHORUS
Love is so hard, too cold, way bold.
Life is crazy, baby, save me.
Take me away from this place, another place, another world.
So I can be another gurl.

I never thought I could trust you again,
Cause your lies were never straight,
And in our fights, I would always win.
Now you're asking me to marry you,
And I don't know what to say.
But I fell back in love with you,
So I'm saying yes today.

CHORUS
Love is so hard, too cold, way bold.
Life is crazy, baby, save me.
Take me away from this place, another place, another world.
So I can be another gurl.

I don't wanna get cold feet, and say hey on our wedding day.
But I'm not going to marry you, you're a nice dude.
I changed my mind, and I don't wanna give you the line.
We can be friends, we can be friends, until the end.

CHORUS
Love is so hard, too cold, way bold.
Life is crazy, baby, save me.
Take me away from this place, another place, another world.
So I can be another gurl.

Allie List, age 14

I wrote this poem when I fell out of love with my boyfriend.

EVERYTHING YOU DO

I love the way

Everything you do

Is annoying to me

I used to think

That fidget was so damn cool

Now I see you

A dog without the magic

Remember when we got along?

I wrote this in dedication to my best friend. She cried when she read it.

MINE TO PROTECT

At night I sometimes have these nightmares
That when I wake you will no longer be there.
In these dreams I see my worst fear—
That someday I may not be there for you.

I remember waking up and finding bloodstains
In the sheets from the night before,
After you sank into that painful retreat.
When you open up
You understand I won't reject you.
But when I hold your wrists too tightly,
I notice that you flinch.
When I see you in pain my heart twists,
But I have to hold in the tears
And keep from you my pain.

I still go to bed with blood-soaked
Images of the pain.
But there is not much more I can do.
I just wish I could be there to help you hold your ground.
Mine to protect, nothing could keep me
From you—except you.

Anna Artyushkina, mentor

During the Journalism Workshop, I wrote about the time I chatted online with a teenage girl on a Russian forum. She reminded me of how lonely adolescents can be and how they desperately need friends and understanding. Young people need moral support and attention—grownups shouldn't forget about them, even when they are preoccupied with their adult concerns.

SOMETHING ABOUT LISA

Would you care to write me a letter?

A letter?? Dumbfounded, my fingers got stuck over the black keyboard with half-erased letters on the keys. Her question caught me off guard. It was a boring rainy day, and I was browsing on a Russian forum somewhere on the World Wide Web. And there she was all of a sudden. Lisa91.

I read your post about Poland and Italy. You must really know geography well.

Not really, I wrote back. I had two teachers at school, one of which was a hysteric woman, and the other—an extraterrestrial guest.

Lol.

I could hear her giggle, I like geography too. But the lessons at school are so boring! I was going to answer, when ...

Would you care to write me a letter??

You don't know me at all. Can I ask you how old you are??

Fourteen.

Something painfully familiar penetrated my heart as I was blankly staring into the glimmering screen.

I have no friends. I am always alone.

I saw myself in between those lines: It was exactly how I was at fourteen, an awkward teenager who is pretending to be sick to make her mother let her stay home only because all the girls have declared a boycott on her. I was afraid of school at times, with its strict teachers, popular girls who would scrutinize my outfit with a slight nod of disgust. And so was Lisa91. Balancing in the waves of the Internet, she came out to ask for help.

I will write you a letter.

I hated myself for that miserable lie at the moment. What would I write her about? What could a frustrated adult entangled in her life like a spider in its own cobweb possibly tell her about?

Sometimes I don't have anyone to talk to. Maybe we could write each other letters. I promise I will answer right away. I won't be boring, I promise. You can write about anything—music, books, geography. I am a curious kid. I only have problems with math ...fractions aren't easy...

I got up and went to the kitchen to make a cup of strong coffee. The rain was still bombarding the window with billions of sonorous drops. I thought of Saint-Exupery and his Little Prince. I was thinking about his simple secret: "It's only with the heart that one can see rightly, what is essential is invisible to the eye." The pilot, suffering from the heat and lack of water, by a broken plane in the middle of a desert, saw a little child who told him about the essential in the world. When you give yourself, you receive more than you give. And now I was responsible for what I had tamed, intentionally or not. I was responsible for my rose. I went back to the bedroom and made my black keys with half-erased letters dance under my fingertips again.

Dear Lisa!

Mara Bochenek, age 16

During the Creative Nonfiction Workshop, I wrote this poem about a guy at school who I can't stand.

THE WONDERFUL WORLD OF HIGH SCHOOL

Walks around like he owns the world.

Thinks he can walk over everyone because of his good looks.

Talks about how much he spent

On a Louis Vuitton wallet that turned out to be fake.

Carries around pictures of his model girlfriend,

But tells everyone she's not

His girlfriend.

Never does his homework, always asks to copy.

Breathes really loud, wheezes when he breathes.

Comes to school every morning tired, complaining he got home too late.

Thinks all the teachers love him so much that they raise his grade so he's passing.

Always late for school.

Gets really close to a teacher and talks really low,

Giving a lame excuse to try to get out of detention.

Tells everyone he was on a show on MTV.

Turns out he lied, it was really on the N.

Got mad at me

Because I told the truth.

Christina Barba, age 18

I submitted a poem called "Our Pens Speak for Us" and was asked if I could rewrite it as a nonfiction piece. I decided to shift the theme from the power of writing to the power of friendship. True friendship has always been something I have searched for, and I found it when my friend and I started this notebook.

FRIENDSHIP IN INK

I've always been the girl with friend problems. Many times I've been lied to, abandoned, manipulated and betrayed, and it seemed like it would never change. I finally cracked after my last toxic friendship at the end of freshman year. I felt like a total and utter reject, a permanently defective person who was just incapable of finding a decent friend. I shut down from other girls. If no one came near me, no one could hurt me.

Ironically, I still ached for someone, ANYONE, to be a friend to me. I transferred out of my private high school into public school for my senior year because we couldn't afford the tuition anymore. I thought, "If I find a companion, great. If not, at least I'm used to being a lonely girl at lunch."

That's when I met Sheena. My first day at my new school, I ate lunch alone against a wall. As I ate my sandwich, I saw her walking by and we made eye contact. The next day in French, she asked me to eat lunch with her. I instantly felt so welcomed despite old feelings of fear and uncertainty. Over time, we became very close, discovering our similarities.

We're both the only child and we've both struggled to find people whom we could truly call "friends." I realized she was another version of me, and I was so happy that I wasn't the only one. So we became true friends. One day, Sheena suggested we start a notebook and write to each other back and forth. So she bought a cute little notebook and decorated it. When I read what she wrote in her first entry, I was taken aback by how she poured herself out in the ink. I didn't realize how much she valued me, how much pain she was in. She never conveyed this magnitude of emotion in her everyday speech and personality. It was overwhelming. So I wrote back with equal fervency, and our notebook was born.

It became apparent to me how much we write that we don't say out loud. We just let everything out. We pick up on each other's unspoken thoughts, the things we write out instead of talking about them. Both of us are going through difficult times and we use those pages to vent to each other. It's a powerful experience to write from the heart and expose that piece of yourself to another. We share our vulnerability when we read what the other has written.

Sheena and I have a unique friendship. We constantly write about our hurt and struggles and we encourage each other with positive, supportive feedback. Our friendship is based on baring ourselves to one another, protecting each other from a world that has given us painful experiences and nurturing the great qualities we see in each other. There is magic in our pens, and it manifests itself in our notebook and in our friendship.

Lily Mendoza, age 16

CHILL

What is this that I feel?

I don't understand

I feel this chill around my body

Every time I think about you.

I can't feel this way

What is this that I feel?

It can't be love

Because I can't love you.

Allie List, age 14

I wrote this as a way to deal with the pain of losing a friend.

ONCE THEY WERE THE BEST OF FRIENDS

You can feel enmity not by sharp glances or cruel words,

But by the cool cheekiness of being ignored,

That would be the goal—more effective hatred makes better love—

Or something.

Maybe all it does is further the hurt,

Each betrayal ten times worse

Than the next

And the last,

Though the first was the most amplified.

The more you can add, the more it digs deep.

Enemies, once they were the best of friends,

True-blue, dude-loving, note-writing sisters

Turned bitter,

In the right mood it's bittersweet,

But that's a little bit rare now.

Think of the things

That could have been.

Mara Bochenek, age 16

I wrote this when I was mad at my friend. It's not your typical girl's poem about her good friend.

SHE

I'm sitting here wondering
to myself:
She thinks she's the best.
She thinks she's smarter than me.
She thinks she has found perfect love.
But in retrospect
she's just like everyone else,
trying to make it in the world.
Why do we have to be like this?
Can't we all just agree
that no one is perfect, no one is best?
There is always going to be
someone out there who is smarter.
Can't we just stop?
Stop comparing whose love is greater
or who will find perfect love first?
But then I realize
the world doesn't always agree.
Not everyone can always agree
on everything.

Melina's mentor Jayna Rust: *"Melina never wrote a poem until the first WriteGirl workshop this season. She didn't seem too thrilled about it at the time, but she really began to like it. She started emailing me poems that she would randomly write. This is the first one she wrote on her own."*

SHADOW

I am just your shadow
following you everywhere

I do what you do
just to please you

You stand
And the hatred that comes from your eyes
It burns

You blame me for everything
While all I try to do is please you

Lovely Umayam, age 17

I was inspired by the snippets of true stories that everyone wrote on posters around the room at the Creative Nonfiction Workshop. I took some bits from other people's stories and created this one.

RAINY DAY

Yes, holding hands during a rainy day as fingertips whisper sweet nothings against fingertips, entangling love within the small bond, kissing, making love while rain just falls limp against our knuckles, overpowering what we had.

Remember that? That day when you took me out to Costco in the middle of a storm, just to buy me a chicken wrap because all I ate for breakfast was a scoop of Fruit Loops? The fact that you kept on kissing my wet cheeks, brushing rain away, to keep me smiling, telling me not to go hungry just yet, that it would all be fine after that chicken wrap?

We walked as if we were men on the moon, so slow, so eloquent, so in love, while everyone passed by with newspapers on their heads and Technicolor umbrellas in their hands to thwart the rain. We welcomed it, like we didn't care, like we were really in love, like it wasn't a game. To you, it was only a game—a waiting game.

Karen Girard, mentor

I wrote this about two friends. Each of them was wonderful, but together they were terrible. In admiring how Rebecca re-imagined herself after the break up, I realized that sometimes the most compelling stories are the ones right in front of us.

REBECCA AND GENE

Because he wanted her to
She changed
Her hair
Her friends
Her sheets
Her routine
Her opinions
Herself
Until she didn't recognize
Herself anymore.

A sliver of herself saw
He'd never be happy
With her or for her
He was a pair of shoes
Two sizes too small
So she changed
Her lipstick
Her apartment
Her habits
Her job
Her life
So that she could
Take back
herself.

Everyday

Heroes

TRIBUTE

A friend of mine inspires me.
While she's constantly trying to make the world a better place,
she already **is** a better place.

This city is full of exceptional women, some of whom bake delicious cupcakes!

I felt disillusioned when Christopher Reeve died. He was a paradigm for human strength and mental endurance. As the weeks went by, I realized that life is fragile and that we are vulnerable almost every day of our lives. Heroes are everywhere, and this poem is a thanks to the heroes in our everyday lives.

THE DAY SUPERMAN DIED

What happened the day that Superman died?
The Man of Steel succumbed,
Fell to his knees.
Villains arose, hope grew dim.
He was the strongest man, it had seemed.

What happened the day the tsunami occurred?
Mother Nature was disturbed,
Tears dropped, the water fled.
Spirits were broken as the death toll rose.

What happened the day the tabloids exposed
That the "perfect marriage" could inevitably grow old?
Love as a foundation,
Love as a lock.
The tabloids proved otherwise,
Love was a crock.

On my way to school today, the radio blurred
Atwater Village, a train wreck occurred.
People dead on their way to work,
Bodies tangled in the mess,
Faith in God diminished.
We were children of a lesser unknown.

Yet through all the rubble,
Through the veil of unpleasant fog.
Our world possessed a foundation after all.
United we will rebuild, on devastated soil,
Divided we find only solitude.
The sun made its way across the sky that afternoon.

But then again, nobody ever did forget
The day that Superman died.

Allison Deegan, mentor

I wrote this piece about a WriteGirl mentee. She begins college in the fall and her new community is in for a few surprises.

CARLISLE

There will be a different bend to the light spectrum on the day that she arrives. There will be a faint shift in the wind, a rustling barely audible in the woods just outside town. Deer, hawks, instincts sharp and hopeful, will sense her addition to the landscape. They will recognize her song as truth, nature, fellowship. She is coming to Carlisle and nothing will ever sound the same.

The J. Crew socialites and pseudo-internationals will stand at a distance at first, scratching their heads on the quad and at the coffee shops. They will scrutinize her long, wavy, gleaming hair. They will wonder why their reflected glory appears to fade. They will never figure out who she really is and they will be the lesser for it. She is coming to Carlisle and they won't know what they've missed.

The professors and ponderers will embrace the electricity in the air and understand that a new discovery has just entered their orbit. They will see her resolve as a force to be reckoned with and try to latch onto her. They will investigate, entertain, cajole and try to unlock all of her mysteries. They may unlock a few. She is coming to Carlisle and her answers are what they have been searching for.

The revolutionary war ghosts and Washington exiles will confer in quiet rebellion, wondering if something can be done about her. They will cower in the presence of her bright and rising consciousness, fearing change. They will form a committee to study the problem but will never arrive at a solution. There is no solution. She is coming to Carlisle and they will never be able to quiet her.

When a very famous Filipino actor died, his funeral was televised for hours on Philippine television. As I watched, I thought about what he had imagined his journey to his final rest would be and the spectacle his service had become.

A FUNERAL

How would you feel if thousands of people came to your funeral? Happy? Sad? Frustrated? A bit claustrophobic maybe? All you see is darkness, the lid of your coffin. But you don't see the outside world filled with your devoted and drunk fans, screaming your name like it will raise you from the dead.

Your quiet path to your last mound is suddenly disturbed, as it becomes a never-ending march to heaven since your carriage moves about three miles per hour. People around you are overwhelmed with emotion and exuberance, singing the national anthem sluggishly, throwing magnolias at your shining tomb, drowning from their own perspiration just to see a glimpse of your sobbing wife while the center of attention is you: cold, unmoving, detached. The stairway to heaven becomes more like a trip to Vegas.

Four hours are gone and you are still making your way to the funeral and still surrounded by drones of people wanting to be a part of something historical. The horse already gave up on you, yet your family never faltered, carrying your casket by the shoulder and walking you to your grave. God is looking down on you, too, making sure your white glistening glory doesn't fall as your bearers are pushed and shoved by your mob. Even in your death, you're still encircled with the buzz of life, of cameras.

If you could just hear, you'd be deaf with the noise around you. If you could just feel, you'd be aggravated with the disrespect your loyal fans are showing. If you could just scream, you'd probably make everyone stop and go home. But you can't. So where are you in all this? Nowhere. You're maybe just watching invisibly, shaking your head to the crowd. You are shocked at the fact that in the end, you are still all glamour, that your personal movie reel hasn't ended, that people are craving more. This isn't how people should go. This isn't peace.

Zoe Beyer, age 16

I wrote this during a mentoring session with Claire. I had only known her for about a month and I was a little embarrassed to write a poem about her! I had never really realized the things that I admired in Claire until I sat down to write a poem about her. She has so many amazing qualities, and we have so many things in common. She is twenty-six and I am sixteen, but sometimes I think we're the same person!

CLAIRE

Those feelings of peculiar intensity
that I have not yet experienced—
The thrill of being in limbo,
of knowing all the answers
but still stopping to ask for directions.
The fear of making your own life,
of being alone,
making muffins from scratch.
That anxiousness—waiting for the world to happen
miraculously,
as if the pieces will one moment unroll into your lap.

I can't imagine, the idea
of not knowing when my day would begin and end.
I envy that feeling of anticipation,
of suspension,
dangling,
but with purpose.
And I wait for the moment when a breeze
will float through my shirt, lifting me,
because I know you are never so self-aware
as the moment when the wind blows the bangs across your face.

ZOE

That ferocity.
Speeding down the 10, the freedom
of driving herself to the edge of the continent.
Breaking air for the first time in her life
but not the last. Sylph, a woman mouths
and I sharpen when I read the word.
How dare she? I can feel it in my muscles,
this instinct. Then I remember whom I dared
to be when I was Zoe.

Los Angeles, a series of lights and whispers
just barely outside of this moment.
She likes the curves, the care and the constant
attention they require. It's on the straight ways
that she begins to wander. I want to tell her
that the cliffs can be addictive, like pain.
Long stretches of tidy lines, like driving
through Kansas at 18, will be harder to face
than she thinks. Squint, I'll say, and even the fields
will bend.

Shauna Smith, mentor

In a workshop, we had to write about people or things that inspire us, and I thought of Phoolan Devi and her unyielding spirit. Devi was born into a lower caste in India. She joined and later led a gang of bandits who targeted the corrupt upper class and became a champion of the poor. After years as an outlaw, she turned herself in and endured eleven years in prison. By 2001, she was becoming a major force in Indian politics and had just been elected to Parliament when she was assassinated.

FOR DEVI

Devi, Bandit Queen, a modern heroine.

People's hero. Women's hero. Victim. Phoenix. Avenger.

Martyr.

Some say she was a Robin Hood, a Billy the Kid.

A romanticized villain, a common thug.

>   *What else will they name you*

>   *now that you're gone?*

They think they silenced her voice

but they only expanded her reach.

>   *Your final scream reached farther than ever before.*

>   *And now people are listening, now they are looking.*

The world was shocked and saddened

even for one so wild, so vicious in her own right.

>   *But somewhere you must have known*

>   *that there are no happy endings*

>   *for lower-caste flower goddesses.*

With spirit born of violence, her destiny led her

to violent end.

But she knew that would be the way

when she started that path.

>   *You knew your end would meet you soon enough—*

>   *You just hoped the fight in you would last long enough*

>   *to see change come.*

It was time to shake the ancient Indian dust from society's antiquated ideas

about women, about castes, about humanity.

No—she was not granted enough time

to finish what she started.

But it was long enough

for her

to endure.

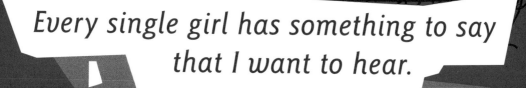

The Thrill

SELF

# of Being

I have found that writing can help me express myself even better than speaking!

Poetry is louder than I thought!
Speak it, sisters!

I look forward to telling a story that makes people feel like it's ok to be flawed.

Shawna's mentor, Lexa Houska: *"Shawna is so open and friendly that I forget she has a dark side. But I think we all have that and need our own secret place to hide out. I think this poem has a very universal quality and really speaks to young women."*

SECRET ROOM

There is a secret room in my heart.
There is a broken mirror because I think I'm ugly.
I smashed the clock because I hate change.
I'm afraid of the future.

I have a key to this secret room.
It's a password.
I'm not telling.
It's mine.

My secret room has a cabinet.
Paints for streaking the walls with my frustration.
Journals for writing letters that will not be read.
Please don't touch.

I have a book called *Alice in Wonderland*.
A girl fell down a rabbit hole.
She discovered a beautiful garden.
She painted roses.

I remember now.
I fell down a rabbit hole too.
I discovered my special place.
But I like my roses to be normal.

I've learned that there is always a reason to be thankful.

ME AND MY GLASS EYE

Two years ago, during a routine eye exam, my doctor casually told me that I had a cataract in my right eye. Suddenly, my mind was flooded with questions. Don't only old people get cataracts? Wait, what is a cataract? And how did I develop it? To the last question my doctor just shrugged and said, "I don't know." She didn't know? She didn't know? All those fancy degrees and certificates on her wall and she didn't know? Those three cold, insensitive words still lingered in the air when she decided to add to them. "Were you hit really hard in the eye recently?" I said, "No." She asked, "Are you sure?"

Okay, I'm no genius, but I think I'd remember being hit really hard in the eye! Well, unless I was hit in the eye, blacked out and completely forgot that I was hit in the eye. In which case, the doctor's line of questioning would be valid. Perceptive even. Anyway, I went home from her office mad at God. Why my eye? I'm a writer. I need my eyes, both of them. I suddenly imagined dictating my scripts to an assistant, an assistant who ignored everything I said and wrote what she wanted instead. How was I going to know? I was blind!

There had to be some lesson God was teaching me in all this, but I just couldn't see it. (No pun intended.) Fast forward six months. Fluorescent lights whisk by overhead as I'm being wheeled into surgery. My throat is dry. My hands are trembling. I want to cry, but the anesthesiologist is cute, so I just smile bashfully. Hey, a girl's gotta do what a girl's gotta do. My doctor says I have nothing to worry about. Within one hour she's going to break my eye lens, suck it out, insert a plastic lens, sew me back up and voila! Twenty-twenty vision. "Feel better?" "No!" The surgery went exactly as planned. Well, except for the part where I woke up in the middle of it. All I remember are people, who looked a lot like trees, hovering over me and my doctor saying, "Don't move." How could I move? My head was strapped to the table and there was a sharp object sticking out of my eye!

It's been a year and a half since I first found out that I had a cataract. And guess what? My doctor was right. I now have perfect vision... and a cool story to share.

During World War II, when the pilots were fired upon, small shards of plastic from their canopy would get lodged in their eyes, but it didn't affect their sight. Miraculously the material was compatible with their eye tissue. This discovery led doctors to use the same material to make artificial lenses. Had this discovery not been made, I'd be walking around with Coke-bottle glasses—designer Coke-bottle glasses, but Coke bottle glasses, nonetheless.

Since my "ordeal" I've met a guy with major eye problems—laser eye surgery gone awry. Now he has to wear a permanent glass contact. It's painful. He can't even make his own tears. When he told me his story I actually thanked God I only had a cataract. Who knew I'd be thankful for something I was so mad about earlier? Hey, I think I just figured out the lesson in all this. In every situation, good or bad, you can always find a reason to be thankful.

This piece was inspired by one of Laura Aguilar's photographs. It brought up many emotions and made me think about how I view myself and how others view me.

LAURA AGUILAR

Forgive me, for I am not the woman you want to sell.

Forgive my shape, for I am not the woman you want me to be.

Forgive me, for making you stop and think, for I am more than fat,

more than anyone can label me.

Forgive me, for I am the woman that has chosen to forgive you.

I forgive you for looking at me, undressing me, and I even forgive you

for the first thought in your head being "she's a fatass."

I forgive you, for I am more than a fatass, I am me:

A woman of forgiveness

A woman of pride

Of pride in myself

My body

Incredible pride

For I am me

Nothing you can sell or buy, nothing typical,

Someone you can love, someone that can make you think.

But on top of everything,

I am me, a woman of forgiveness.

I wrote this in my early twenties when I was feeling conflicted about my future and isolated from my family and friends in Ohio. I felt like the artist in me was dying. Leaving Ohio for California helped me recover my artistic voice.

NOTHINGNESS

People take and take and take from me
not with malicious intent, I know
but because they've received my invitation.
I settle, with a shudder, into exhaustion
after hours of seeing myself peel away.
Comforting words march by me,
a syntactical battalion poised and perfect and prepared to fight
But demons arise, whose sticks and stones do break bones,
whose words, like armaments, shell the unshielded fortress
Ancient, chastising voices bring dread in their reminder:
tainted souls are for feeding.
The tortured ones cannot grow from the gifts they possess.
Their guarded wisdom, sleeping soundly like the pit of a peach,
is snatched greedily from the bruised flesh that protects.
Once scar tissue, covering bloodless wounds, boasted girth
fat enough to pry the teeth of zippers.
Now there is only a terrible translucence
where bones used to live, blood used to flow and skin used to stretch.
I could pass my finger through it to confirm the apparition,
if I still had a finger—they were the last to go
And I am struck dumb at the nothingness that is me.

Katherine Taylor, mentor

I wrote this during a writing session with my mentee, Stephanie, at the McDonald's on 7th and Alameda.

TWELVE MINUTES IN THE LIFE OF THE FICTIONAL KATHERINE TAYLOR

I type seven lines of dialogue and delete four. I read several pages of *The Sun Also Rises* and decide that my dialogue is very bad, but I continue to write more anyway. I read more of *The Sun Also Rises* and delete everything I have written. I check my email, and if there is a message from my funny friend Bruce, I respond immediately. If there is a message from my demanding friend Enid, I delete it. If there is a message from my interesting and kind but difficult friend Martin, I wait and think about what to respond until tomorrow. I drink flavored water and feel very bad about spending so much money on flavored water.

I look at my magazine galleys to remind myself that I can write decent dialogue when I try very hard and do not procrastinate and do not drive to Trader Joe's every time I run out of flavored water. I check the Internet for a history of recent earthquakes. I look at the wall and wait for an earthquake. No earthquake comes.

Liliana Olivares-Perez, mentor

My job and my extracurricular activities don't leave much time or energy for myself. I haven't written in a while and this has caused me to think about what would happen to me if I didn't have writing in my life.

THE TRUTH ABOUT BANK TELLERS

I can't remember the last time I sat down to write, fingertips on the keyboard, door closed, soundtrack of choice softly providing inspiration. It scares me. It scares me that I might forget. It scares me that my creative mind is growing flabby and weak.

"Make time for it," people say. But when? I'm too busy being a "responsible adult," driving, working, worrying, earning, paying, owning, striving. I wonder, if I let it go, who will I become? If I let it go, will my being change? My walk, my talk, my laugh, my scowl, are they so intertwined?

Hey, you, unbearable bank teller. You with the knotted face. Why do you hate life so? Is it because as you count dollars, touch coins, you see it, hidden in your closet behind the winter coats and wrapping paper—that canvas, unfinished, dusty, rotting, forgotten? You see that part of your life you exchanged for stability, 401(k), health insurance and greed? And now, disgruntled, you hand me my bank slip.

I take it, put it in my purse, walk out into the bright sunlight and slip into my car, my green metal cocoon. I sit down and my heart sinks. I just saw the future, my future, ten years from now. But then, I see a pen and a piece of paper. I grab them and I start scribbling away. I furiously purge myself, my soul and I know that it can't be put away, that it can't leave me. It needs me as much as I need it.

Elena Karina Byrne, mentor

I wanted to capture the feeling of anxiety one musters in order to write and re-create.

A RECIPE FOR ANXIETY

"Literature is achieved anxiety."
     —Harold Bloom

Hitching a ride on your heartache, exile the calendar's numbers
to the dirt-end of the road's turn. Set aside days for whispering in
your own ear, years for going astray. Sending all open vowels out
the window of your mouth, keep the consonants for your teeth.
Occasion hell when an advance of ideas runs amuck up
your spine. Take four quarts longing and a pinch of Epsom
salt to the family table. Spread out a wreckage of syntax
and let cool overnight. Wielding a hot quill, write, write,
every morning, a letter to yourself under the bed. Pray
to the chain gang of childhood that never let you go.
While reciting the Cosmologist's alphabet, say something
back to yourself, in your sleep. Without telling anyone, rescue
all the half-crayons you can, and take them home as an alchemy
for painting. Launch a page of gray carrier pigeons
toward the past. Now, blindfolded, walk backwards. Undiluted,
walk forwards into the blue requiem of ocean. Then know
how far to walk the sign language of sadness.

Angela Martinez, age 17

THE WORLD

I'm not a person who judges
I'm not a person who criticizes
I'm not a person who even lies
I'm a person who gives from the heart

CHORUS
I live in a world of judgment
In a place where no one cares
I live in secret, an empty cave
That shuts me out from what's there

I see the world with much damage
Even see the angels crying
I ask for help, it doesn't come
Why is the world tearing apart?

CHORUS
I live in a world of judgment
In a place where no one cares
I live in secret, an empty cave
That shuts me out from what's there

I live in a world of judgment
In a place where no one cares
I will open my arms and break free

Elizabeth Gill, mentor

This poem expresses a feeling I've had all my life that I can't quite put into words exactly what I want to say. People close to me have often said, "It's like you're just about to say something earth-shattering... but you never quite do." Perhaps this is why I write though—looking for the magic words!

BLUE WOMAN'S APOLOGIA

Blue Woman has trouble finishing
her sentences, she speaks
before thinking and gets
caught
with her pants half-down
even though she's already
naked

some wonder if

she simply forgets
what she's going
to say, like
an animal in a fairy
tale given
speech, then
made dumb
by some witch out for
a purple laugh

many have accused

her of leading them
on (sometimes for
years) to the brink
of some
brilliant view.
Blue Woman admits
she gets
frustrated trying
to pluck stars
which tend to melt on the tongue
so no one believes you
know what you're

talking about.

Lena Brooks, age 16

I wrote this poem after a bout of loud, badly-timed talking.

8:32

Prone to spells of loud talking and incidents
that have names. My voice catches
like fast and heated motors,
catches like Detroit and the words sucked deep
roll up and out my throat:
fast fast fast.
And when I talk I hold my face
in my hands. My fingers hold full pupils
like trash bags full of song.
And I sing like a hollow room,
"Don't look in my direction one more time or
I will throw my garbaged language
like nothing and for no use."
I will use the last of my sense
in losing all of meaning.
I will become only a hallucination,
only a tube of light for your bad looks.
Wholly nothing like the candle fire
when the fuel is full.
Clean and leaping like a girl on one foot
who fell down gracefully.

Dinah Coronado, age 15

I wrote this after I had been through the worst experience and still came out a stronger person, a stronger writer, a stronger Dinah.

I'VE BEEN THIS

Where do I go from here?
I've been sad and angry
I've been there
How do I start from the past?
Wrong and mistrusted
I've been an outcast
What do I do to make things right?
Weak and weary
I've been cursed to fight
Who do I have to blame?
Judged and persecuted
I've been thrown in the game
Why do I cry?
Hurt and pushed
I've been asking why
Now what do I have to do?
I've been locked down and captured
Hiding from you
Where do you go from me?
Weird and crazy
I've been what you see

Julia Guest, age 16

This piece essentially focuses on the judgments people make about each other. Through writing this song, I learned more about myself, and I was finally able to put my feelings about this issue into words.

WALK WITH ME

Pretend like you know me, I won't say a thing
Try to control me, but you will not win
Tell me you're sorry
Seems like the only way this will end

CHORUS
Maybe I'm unpredictable
So what if I'm so unusual
Observe me for a day
But walk with me all the way

That day I felt quiet, didn't have much to say
Will all your friends remember me that way?
I hate that they judge me
They barely know me anyway

Talk to me and see that I'm not everything you made me up to be
I've proved your assumptions wrong
I've been a different girl all along

CHORUS
Maybe I'm unpredictable
So what if I'm so unusual
Observe me for a day
I'm just what God has planned

Deborah Bramwell, age 15

When I started this piece, I meant to write about mourning. At first Molly's mourning was very mainstream, but the piece refused to be written because Molly's mourning should not have been mainstream. At the time I was volunteering at a middle school, and I had forgotten to bring a lunch. So there I was, thinking about mourning and licking strawberry syrup off my fingers. This is from a larger piece about family.

DIFFUSION

The eventual morning clamor of the students attending summer workshops woke her; she slipped out of bed and went to the vending machines wearing nothing but an oversized T-shirt and twisted knickers. Every morning she bought a Coke and a pack of Pop-Tarts. She didn't always eat the sugary cookies, but would pop the Coke open and fall into bed. Hours passed the shadows over her; one syrupy sip at a time she drank her can of soda, pretending she was adrift on a raft at sea. She floated and listened to the waves lap lazily against her raft. The Coke kept her alive. Repeatedly, Molly survived.

On better days, when the salty sea had yet to touch her lips, Molly awoke with the energy for emotion. With any notebook and pen she could grab, she scribbled angry letters to her mother. Pages overflowed with vulgarity and condemnation. To her eldest brother, five years her senior, Molly penned accusatory notes calling him a doormat, a coward, unfit to be a brother.

"You are my brother," she later remembered writing. "Why aren't you looking after me? Why weren't you looking after Tommy?"

Letters to Tom did not come so easily. He had never lied. She had nothing to condemn him for. Every half-begun letter brought her oceans of tears she could ill afford, and she had to bite her lip and take a sip of boiling Coke to keep from crying.

Surviving at sea means not losing a single drop of water. Survivors never cry.

Molly had to buy the Pop-Tarts with red filling. The package read "Strawberry." When the goo dribbled over her fingers or her chin, she knew it was the blood of whatever dead fish had floated to her raft. The nutrients in the blood were precious, and Molly licked it off her skin before it could leave a stain.

She remembered the ancient Celts who drank the blood of their enemies, of horses, to gain their strength. In waking dreams she swallowed a fox's cunning, a shark's jaws, the fish's breath in the water. She awoke on the floor, drowning.

And so her raft avoided a different tide.

Molly stopped leaving her room. She had enough Cokes and strawberry Pop-Tarts to keep her alive. Laying slovenly on her bed in the day, she feared the sunlight would blacken her organs. At night she felt her teeth grow long and licked congealed strawberry blood from bland, sugary pastry shells.

Time passed, and Molly found herself sleeping later into the morning. Mornings melted into afternoons. Every night, in the gentle moonlight, life seemed just bearable, and she thought of walking on the quad. She imagined the dewy grass beneath her feet, the wind on her skin, fresh air in her lungs. Occasionally she reached the door, where she would pause, an unidentified enormity sitting on her chest, and, as always, she turned around.

Karly Abreu, age 14

I was experimenting with song lyrics that rhymed, but then I realized this piece was meant to be a poem.

PLAYED

I'm sick of crying
I'm tired of trying
I'm over this thing
I want it to get over me.
I'm through with hurting
I'm over with blurting
everything I don't mean to the wind.
I'm no longer just going to be a puppet
Because I'm tired of being played a fool.
I'm human, not the court jester.
Step aside.
Let me through.
I'm never again gonna hurt myself on purpose
With the intention of letting someone see.
I'm not going to watch my emotions run away,
leaving my soul far behind.
I'm tired of being
Played as a fool
Used like a tool
Stored like an email.
I'm human!
Not the court jester.

Judgmental people in my life inspired me to write this piece.

MORE LIKE ME

I wish I were more like me

The person you see me to be

And I've heard it all

Trust me

I wish I really were this mean, heartless

Chick that everybody sees

This evil reflection that everyone sees

This girl that has no cares or feelings

Might sound ironic but I wish I were she

I wish I could look you in the eyes as if you have no effect on me

I wish I were as miserable as you think me to be

You got something twisted cuz that's not me

Just because I don't walk around smiling

In your face doesn't make me unhappy

You judge as if you know

But you know nothing of what goes on internally

Let me tell you something

You see me every day

But you know nothing about me

The girl you see

The one I'm supposed to be

She seems strong with a high level of apathy

She has it easy

I wish I were more like me

But I'm glad you think she's me and I am she

Because it makes it obvious you know nothing about me

This piece was inspired by a Guillermo Gomez Peña photograph. It tied into my current attitude, feeling like I'm more Guatemalan than American, and provoked a lot of reflection about where I fit in the world.

GUILLERMO GOMEZ PEÑA

Shut me out

The world my oyster?

The American dream?

Lies, lies, lies.

Just shut me out.

Without a place

Found in nightmares.

Spare me Mr. God,

Just lie to me

Everything will be fine.

The world is my oyster

Just shut me out

Don't want to hear it, see it or feel it anymore.

Quiet silence, no more.

That's all I desire.

Just shut me out

I'm here yet nowhere, seen but invisible,

Heard but mute.

Colorless, nationless, no one, nothing,

Yet all me.

Glass ceilings everywhere I turn,

Nothing really mine

These bonds, this rug, nothing mine.

Covered with shame of not being you or him or her.

Painful disgust with myself

For not owning that car, that house,

That knowledge.

Spare me Mr. God,

All I want is that oyster to shut myself out of this world,

This box where the walls are closing in on me

And everything is coming to get me.

What is it?

Is it quiet, no more...

Does anybody care?

Am I gone

It's done

Here I am not

No more.

LIFE AS A CHEERLEADER

Everyone says cheerleading is not a sport. Cheer is a sport. We work out, we sweat. We throw people in the air. We catch them. We carry them. We bleed. We suffer injuries as badly as the football players. We can break arms, legs and get head injuries. We practice as hard as they do, As long as they do.

Football season only lasts for a few months, but cheer goes on all year. Football players have a season to prove their worth—in competition, we get three minutes. And football players don't have to worry about losing points for not smiling.

Everyone says cheerleaders are dumb. But to continue on the squad, we need to get good grades.

Cheer is a sport. Just with all girls, in our own way.

Dinah Coronado, age 15

THE WRONG GIRL

I am too fat and too thin to be with you.

I am too happy and too sad to make you smile like I used to.

I am too strange and normal to be what you want me to be.

I am too serious and funny to see what you want me to see.

I am too punk and pop to rock like you.

I am too safe and sexy to be different to be one of the few.

I am too scared and sure to be the perfect girlfriend.

I am too stupid and lame to see that we have come to an end.

I am too pretty and ugly to be the perfect dream.

I am too boring and smoking to give you all of me.

I am too much of a writer and Dinah to let this man change me.

I was inspired to write this after noticing that I am changing, growing into who I will be, who I am, and it's confusing for my family.

HOW DO YOU SAY DICHOTOMY IN TAGALOG?

Every time I pin a flower to my hair,
slip dangling chandeliers on my ears,
put on American clothes,
my father claims to see through it.
He calls me "Hollywood,"
a fake, flashy flesh of a soul,
attempting to shed my true identity,
piecing together a puzzle of Americano Skin
to hide the Cayumangi of my Pilipino.

Is this true?

He thinks I've become an American Zombie;
Never home on weekends,
Skipping hapunan for homework that's been
Stressin' my soul,
the daughter who has come
to hate the Bush Administration's
diabolitics, but has only a vague
perception of who Jose Rizal is
and what El Filibusterismo is all about.

The daughter who uses the eloquence of America,
Pressing, palpable, esoteric words,
But doesn't know the meaning of
nagpapadama, nagpapahiwatig, and nagpapagising.

Is that me?

Trapped between two worlds
Like a mime outgrowing silent tricks,
Wanting to step into the noise,
But stuck between endless, invisible walls,
Left to feel the door with bare palms.

Hard as it may seem, I will find identity.
If I have to, I will march to two different beats of
Two different drums.

I am Hollywood,
With a Tagalog heart.

Ha! Ha!

Ha!

The laughter thundered through the room!

I will fake it
'til I make it,
Even if I break it.

Stephanie Lopez, age 17

I thought it would be fun to write a story from the point of view of a character in a fairy tale.

GRANNY'S STEW

I'm trotting through the darn woods looking for Granny's house. I heard Little Red Riding Hood was coming today. I finally have a chance to tell her my true feelings. I start to trot faster when I see her house. I walk right to the door and kick it with my back leg. "Why, hello, darling! Come in! Little Red Riding Hood will be here any minute," said Granny. "Oh, I'm making some beef stew. Would you like some?" "Of course!" I sit like a good boy and wait to be served. All of a sudden, Granny slips and falls, knocking the stew all over her. I start to lick her face trying to wake her up. "Mmm, this tastes so good." I continue to eat the stew off her. When my belly is full I look down. "Oh my god! I accidentally ate Granny! Little Red Riding Hood will be here any minute!" I quickly run and put on Granny's clothes and jump into bed. Maybe I can fool Little Red Riding Hood and she will still want to be my girlfriend. Just maybe.

Rayline's mentor, Dana Valenzuela: *"Rayline lives outside of the city in a more rural community so she is really in touch with nature. When she read this to me over the telephone, we both cracked up. As we trust each other and laugh more together, we're learning to write more challenging pieces."*

FLY'S LAST MOMENTS

I found a spider, a little black one

I taught him everything

How to swim, how to walk and even how to run.

But one day I taught him a little too much

And made my little friend,

Who I named George,

Into lunch.

I told him "no," not to eat my friends

This is the way my little story ends.

I wrote this during the Fiction Workshop. Everyone wrote true things about themselves on the wall. We each chose two of them and worked them into a story. Mine were "My cat Antonio" and "My father always agrees with me."

ANTONIO THE CAT

I was walking home from school and when I got to my front door, there was a black and orange cat looking up at me and meowing. I bent down to see whose cat it was, but there was no collar. "You are my cat and I shall call you Antonio. You are Antonio the Cat. Come with me Antonio, for I shall dress you up in a little sequined cocktail dress and take you dancing with me."

My mother walked in to the noise of a sewing machine running very rapidly. "What are you making, sugar lump?" she asked.

"A dress. A wonderful dress for my new friend Antonio. Mother, meet Antonio the Cat. Antonio, this is Mother." Antonio raised his paw and gave her a nice, hard shake of the hand.

Mother, being who she is, was not at all pleased with Antonio.

"Father said I could keep him." Father always agreed with me. But Mother, oh, she went on her rampages.

"I am the mom, and you must do as the mom says." She was not at all pleased. Even though she did compliment the wonderful stitching on the dress.

I couldn't take it anymore, so I left with my little Antonio in that wonderful dress. We left and we danced the night away. And Antonio got three times as many numbers as I did.

Kim Purcell, mentor

I normally write novels, but I learned at the Poetry Workshop that you can say a lot in a few words.

THE PURSE

Bought a black purse

With a Brand Name

Cost three hundred and fifty dollars

Thought it would make me

Feel better.

It didn't.

Lexa Houska, mentor

I wrote this at the WriteGirl Poetry Workshop. I thought about the 99 Cent Store and thought it was a funny and unexpected thing to write a poem about. I learned that poetry doesn't always have to follow meter and rhyme rules.

ONE DOLLAR MORE

Bananas, violets, aspirin, brooms.
What's one dollar more?
Candles, pocketbooks, cat food, pills for all that ails.
Everything in life should cost
Just one dollar more.

I throw down my basket and run for the door.
But then stop and ask myself, what's one dollar more?

I run back to my basket
Hold it to me tight.
Fill it with glittering, shining, inviting
Potatoes, soap, napkins, tin foil paper,
Toilet brushes, placemats, brooms
All begging me,
What's one dollar more?

But what is around the corner?
Who will be there?
A handsome man, shiny, scrubbed and singing
A stray child, lonely and crying with arms outstretched
Or maybe laundry detergent?
That's what I really need.
All for only one dollar more.
(Plus tax.)

Each dollar whispers and lies.
My empty pocket giggles, then sighs.
Now there's no more.

Ariel Edwards-Levy, age 15

While innocently making a cup of tea, the first stanza of this poem popped suddenly into my head. The fact that it was 2 a.m. and that I was severely sleep-deprived probably didn't hurt, either. It was partially inspired by the kind of people who sell fascinatingly mundane things on eBay, and the kind that actually bid on them. After the first few lines, it became somewhat of a challenge, as I had absolutely no idea where I was going with it. Even the most dedicated prose writer needs to shift tactics occasionally.

NOT MY CUP OF TEA

Your half-drunk cup of tea is selling on eBay for thirty dollars.
Your lips have touched it, enthuses the seller—
Who no doubt has a great future selling used cars.
It's like a kiss, second degree!

But it's not a simile, it's a cheap styrofoam cup
With the brim worn down and stained a pallid sepia,
And no matter how long I stare at it, it's no masterpiece.
But it stubbornly resists characterization—
Half-moon impressions of dug-in nails neatly circling the brim,
Earl Grey slopping inside like a lukewarm brown ocean
And it's tea for god's sake, from the nearest Starbucks, and

If you put on boots and went to a landfill
You'd find the used Kleenex of the next Picasso,
The pencil shavings from that kid who's gonna cure cancer
And the broken clock his grandpa threw away this morning,
A hundred pieces of toast that look like Jesus,
And a thousand sheets of crumpled paper that were disposed of by
A thousand yous who never really made it after all.

Some dimwit is going to treasure that thing for her whole damn life.

Liliana Olivares-Perez, mentor

As part of my new HR job, I have to write all sorts of emails. This email got lots of responses back from people in the office. I can still have a voice and my personality in something as banal as an office email.

YOUR MOTHER DOESN'T WORK HERE

From: Liliana Olivares-Perez

Sent: Friday, January, 21 2005, 4:19 p.m.

To: LA Office

Subject: Your Mother Doesn't Work Here

Dear All,

I'm sure everyone has noticed that our kitchen seems to be in a downward spiral of cluttered counters and dirty dishes. While it might not seem like a big deal to some of you, we all have to share this office and it's unfair to those who (rightfully) expect a tidy workplace. Yes, we have a cleaning staff which is responsible for straightening the kitchen; however, this does not happen until we've all gone home for the day. And since Jane has given up on taking care of the kitchen by herself, it's now up to each of you to clean up after yourselves.

Not to worry, this task has been made easier for you: you will now find the dishwasher completely empty first thing every morning. Please place dirty dishes there rather than in the sink and throw your trash in one of the seven trash cans in the kitchen.

We're all in this together, so please be considerate of your fellow coworkers and they will extend you the same courtesy. That or you'll all be asked to eat lunch in your car.

Liliana

P.S. We are in the process of installing security cameras in the office. We will catch you in the act.

I'm no longer pregnant!

I AM STILL PREGNANT

I am still pregnant. It is one day after my due date. I'm in purgatory.

This must be what it's like when the doctor says you have six months to live and then it gets to the six-month point and you are still alive. You'd naturally ask yourself, well, when am I going to die if not now? You'd be halfway alive and halfway dead.

Right now I'm halfway a mother and halfway not. I've been waiting for a major change for months and months, nearly ten to be exact, and then it didn't happen.

Why do they say it could be two weeks early? Really they should tell you that it may come on the due date and up to two weeks later. I mean, who needs a full month window? If I had thought that our baby wouldn't even consider arriving before the due date, I'd surely have more patience now.

That's what I prayed for in my prenatal yoga class today—patience. In the meditation, you cup your hands and you pray for your cup to be filled with whatever you want, be it a quality or skill or even a new car. Yes, you can pray for a new car in yoga class. We have a new car. I need patience.

I sang Wahe Guru, Wahe Guru, Wahe Guru, Wahe Gio—don't ask why Gio, but the whole prayer means something like help me God—and I prayed for my hands to be filled with patience. Of course, my mind kept slipping and I thought about the weird dream I had last night in which I was in a tiny boat rushing downstream away from my drowning children and I didn't have an oar.

The music and the meditation finished. My hands were cupped, presumably filled with patience. But when I uncupped them, the patience must have spilled because I was driving home and this guy in a Corolla was driving so slowly that I wanted to honk my horn and scream out my window, "Hurry up, you horrible, stinking Corolla-driving man."

But then I breathed deeply and remembered about my hand cup and the patience that was filling it. And I thought if I'm a screaming maniac, perhaps this baby will take even longer, think the world isn't a nice place to be, that the mother with the empty patience cup is scary and the womb is much better.

Baby, it is not better. Oh no. It's dark and boring. Come on out. It's way more fun here. People smile at you here and you can eat ice cream.

Oh man. I'm sorry. That doesn't sound very patient, does it? Don't worry, baby. You can take your time. I've got my hand cup and I'm filling it up.

But I will see you soon, won't I?

THE MOTHER HANDLER

I cancelled my trip back east recently because the "mother" anxiety was killing me. I can't stand up to my mother's rapid-fire line of questioning and nagging, even after 39 years of experience.

Then I had an idea... I need a mother handler.

This mother handler would be part Animal Planet crocodile guy and part POW counter-intelligence questioner. I'd send in my advance team to wear her down—reel her in and make her a reasonable person.

Then I'd walk in, release her from her hogtie and blindfold. She'd be so happy to see me, she wouldn't ask me if I had a real job or husband yet.

Karly Abreu, age 14

I saw a balloon bouquet while riding down the freeway one day. I was daydreaming about what it was like to be a balloon flying away. I wrote this in class—I'm always daydreaming during school. The unexpected ending is like the unexpected school bell.

HELIUM HEAD

Floating up towards heaven,

The sky is getting closer to my body.

Drifting towards the great beyond.

Courtesy of a child's idle hand

My fate is secure.

Now I am free, lazily

escaping,

leaving this world far behind...

POP!

Christiane Schull, mentor

A poem to read in one breath.

SIZE MATTERS

The sweater fits a mouse
Not a girl and not a house
It was a failure with the house
But it kept the mouse warm

TRANSFORMATION She

Changes

Keep writing because good things come out of it.

I love when I learn something so new
that it changes the way I think about
something I through I already knew.

Kristin Petersen, mentor

My life was in limbo for several months as I waited for different pieces to fall into place. I was tired of waiting for things to get sorted out, but I was still filled with anticipation.

PROMISING

The streets were full of echoes
and she felt the shadows in her hair,
kissing her cheeks,
circling her legs like cats.
The streets knew her like broken glass
and dandelions in cracks.
And with each step,
each twilight hour,
she knew it was time to go.
When time spun to summer,
with streetlights muted
in the heat and haze,
she would make her escape.

Maria Guerra, age 17

I thought my polar positions of pessimism and positivism should be balanced with some rational thought. I now feel that I've figured enough stuff out to move on to the next section of my life.

DECONSTRUCTED CONCLUSION

I have been told by my closest acquaintances that I am annoyingly introspective and needlessly philosophical. I connect completely unrelated subjects with theories that I think are original but which I later find to be universally known. And although this shatters the idea that I'm somehow unique, I find it comforting that there are others who, like me, become tormented with the most idiotic ideals: like love and the meaning of life. However useless my friends believe philosophizing to be, it has helped me to define a self.

After four years of evolvement and complete confusion, which is occasionally followed by some brief moments of clarity, I can say that I wear my age. Until recently, I didn't feel any closer to adulthood and I actually fought it off with all my strength. I'm now beginning to accept the inevitability of change. Although I know that as I grow older I'll find more answers, I know that it won't matter because the list of questions will just grow longer. And as hopeless as this makes me feel, the prospect of getting the answers to my current questions and my curiosity for what the next questions will be excites me.

So this is what I have learned so far: Life, in the big picture, seems to be completely meaningless at this point in the history of man because we cannot understand purpose or a lack thereof. Those who are religious are infinitely blessed because they are at peace with the big picture. Those who are not are often at war with themselves, like me. "I'm a Romantic." "No! I'm an existentialist." "There has to be a God!" "There can't possibly be a God!" "Aaaaaah!" Isn't life wonderful?

So the immediate answer to the purpose of life seems to be along the lines of family and love and a passion for some sort of art. And among all the things that might seem to you as overly-mentioned aphorisms and painfully annoying clichés, I have found some truth and direction.

Diane-Paula A. Valencia, age 17

We were asked to make a list of what inspires us. I thought about the beauty of people as they evolve—people growing old, parents losing their kids, children facing an unknown future, everyone's fear of losing something, those who give up, those persisting, the pure, the flawed, all the beautiful aspects of being human and evolving.

beautifully human

curling into bed, my head sinking onto her warm worn-down womb, once filled with life, veins still running, selfless blood, her jelly belly soft as a pillow, hearing the gurgle sounds that tickle my ear

laugh lines hidden behind worrisome gray hairs, losing a part of his self, skeptical of the rickety swings his children play, time ticking hands, his wrinkled droopy eyes scurry, spewing out child chewing jokes

the venture out the door, in bloom, the thrashing, thriving cosmic mind, exhausted eyes, tired hands, moving in twists and tangles so hard to release, inevitable faults they wish to stop and keep, beautiful friend in a fury, beautifully human

Erica Drennan, age 16

I wrote a longer piece a few months ago entitled "The Garden," which my mentor and I started revising together. I was frustrated because I knew a lot about my main character, but it wasn't coming out in the piece itself. My mentor gave me some garden passages from D. H. Lawrence so that I could gain some inspiration and insight into how gardens are sometimes used as metaphors.

LILLA

She read in the garden. It was her place, and hers alone. No one would dare invade her haven; no one else in the house could understand such a place. In the garden there were no video games, or cell phones, or televisions that blared Oprah. The garden was a place from worlds past, where the only air traffic was the bees darting from blossom to blossom, and the only incoming calls were the birds returning to their nests.

The garden was her release from the cacophony of modern life. There she could lose herself in its endless, lulling harmony. She bathed in the soothing violet of the pansies whenever life inside the house became too fast. She melted in the smiles of the marigolds when her duties as a nanny for monsters with skateboards almost brought her to tears. When it was all too much, roses would cry alongside her, then the daisies would tickle her chin and bring back her smile.

But it was the lilies that kept her alive inside that unfeeling house. Lilies: so slender and seemingly fragile, yet beautiful and strong. Lilies to whom odes were sung in days long ago, but had managed to survive the harsh passage of time. Lilies, as any gardener will tell you, are never dormant. And yet, she was not a lily. All her life she had been waiting for someone to sweep her off her feet and carry her away. But even a dormant flower must eventually bloom.

This life was hers to lead, no one else's. There were no stakes confining her to this patch of earth. She chose to take on the boldness of the sunflower, the grace of the bluebell, the glow of the buttercup, but most importantly, the resilience of the lily. The world was hers.

She uncrossed her arms and let her petals drink in the love of the sun.

Nadine Levyfield, age 15

I wrote this one day based on a true experience. Usually, I find that I like writing when I'm telling the truth about myself.

SMOKING

When I was in my first year of high school, my New Year's resolution was to become more fit, so I got a gym membership. It was called Dee's Gym, just across from Trader Joe's. Dee was a petite blonde woman who smoked constantly, sitting outside on a red chair next to the steps. Her voice was so leathery that I always thought her good fitness habits were completely undermined by her voracious smoking. One day, I was waiting outside for a ride home from my mom when I saw a pack of cigarettes laying on the stairs. As usual, I sat on the red folding chair and listened to my iPod, waiting for my mom. It was raining, but I was under the awning, so I was covered. Noticing the cigarettes, I looked around to see if anyone was nearby. I heard someone in the office upstairs jiggling their keys and getting ready to lock the door. I saw the cars parked, and no one outside. So I took the pack. Glancing inside, I saw only one cigarette left, so I didn't feel bad about stealing it. I put it in my bag and could smell it. It smelled like it had already been smoked. I shrugged and waited for my mom. When I got home, I couldn't help but notice how bad it still smelled, so I went into the bathroom to take a look. Opening the small white box, all I saw were butts, left inside so they wouldn't get soggy in the ashtray. After that I decided not to smoke.

Jacqueline Hahn, age 15

Nightmares, at least to me, feel real. It takes me a while to realize that they aren't. Writing this piece taught me that no matter how scary something is, time will help you get over it.

NIGHTMARES

My dreams send me to cold barren places where

not even the strongest of lights can pierce through

the eerie darkness.

I cry out for help only to be ignored.

My pathetic tries to escape are laughed at while my soul is constantly tortured

by gruesome images I am forced to watch over and over again.

I can feel tears on my face but I cannot move.

I am immobile.

For a brief moment I am standing on that plane between the dreaming

world and reality.

My vision is disoriented, my breathing ragged and uneven.

I wake up with a cry.

Relief floods my body, warm and welcome like that first sip of hot chocolate

on a cold winter's night, as I realize it's just a dream,

nothing more than a nightmare.

It's interesting how my life bled into this piece of writing. I thought I was just creating a list of descriptions about oranges, but when I looked at it a year later, I saw that on a subconscious level, I had been writing about my divorce.

CONJURER OF ORANGE

piled high on the plate, the citrus globes glowed in the candlelight
faded photographs and incense witness prayers rising

sparrows flittered, leaves clapped. beneath the tree,
a field of decayed mandarins, their skin turned powdery green

you sliced through the middle, revealing clear filaments and yellow seeds
you sliced through the middle, baring parts of me, not yet given

fragrance drifted from the white blossoms in my hair
inside the flowers, tiny green fruits, firm like pearls, were forming

sometimes, we shared peace: plates of carefully arranged slices
between the words and the silence, sweetness disappeared

torrents of mustard-colored bile—pulp and flesh—poured from you

i watched you, nursing your coffee and cigarette on the deck
then, i poured a glass of juice, drank the pale color, bitter the taste

the pith was too thick, winter fruit has no life

my words slurred, the wine pitcher emptied
so only translucent slices, stained a bruised color, remained

on the freeway, a golden orb rolled past me. then,
another bumped against the median. then, i saw them,
rolling, scattering, crushed beneath the bellies of SUVs and sedans

Gaby Cardenas, age 16

I am a member of Curves and one weekend we went to the tallest staircase in Los Angeles. I had a lot of fun, and when I came back home, I just had to write about it! This piece has been by far the most entertaining to perform. I love to make people laugh, and while I still write serious pieces, I can't help but write what comes most naturally to me—humor.

THE JOURNEY ON THE STAIRS

I don't know what inspired me to do this. It sounded like a marvelous idea back then.

Oh, stairs, easy. Four times, shmore times. In fact, it had still sounded like a good idea when we were all huddled up at the foot of the stairs eagerly awaiting the long flight up. All of us started off the same, enthusiastic and energetic.

But stairs have a way of showing you your place. Each step I took and each quavering muscle determined how far I would go. Would I reach the top? My breath was becoming harder to catch by the moment.

The top is closer, closer, getting closer. Just a few more steps... How annoyingly inspirational the will to overcome can be.

My face fell as I realized I was panting like a dog and my mother held the water and she was far, far ahead. Another incentive to keep going? Seconds turned into long, tedious minutes. I needed something, ANYTHING to get my mind off this grueling task. I looked to my sides, trying to enjoy the scenery.

Poison oak. Great, now I have to be careful.

Lost in thought, I suddenly became aware of my surroundings. I could hear voices now, getting closer, getting louder.

"You did it!"

"You're almost there!"

"Come on!"

"Keep going!"

As I reached the last step, I looked up and found that the end had come at last. Weary, I trudged over to my mother asking for water. Why did I do this again? "Turn around" was my answer. And turn around I did. The view was spectacular.

My breath hitched in my throat. "This was almost worth it." I gasped.

"Good," my mother replied. "Now let's do it three more times."

Poetry is the music inside of a person.

Fireflies

in My Hand

PHILOSOPHICAL

There is a song inside everyone.

Depending on how one writes,
real life can be like a fairy tale.

Ashtynn Baltimore, age 13

I wrote this in a Starbucks at a session with my mentor. Sometimes people overlook things that are important in life.

OVERLOOKED THINGS

There's a lot to pens that people just don't pay attention to. They're all just so mysterious. Pens with five different colors, a pen that is supposed to be black that's blue. A sense of mystery and sensation at the same time. They hold everything that gets held back. Your opinions, thoughts, views. The secrets that are so hard to confess to someone. The only thing you can trust. Paper could give it away. Someone finds it and there's no going back. No way to take back the reality. Pens let you express your true self, not the things people make you out to be. They allow you to be someone you don't want to be. Be colorful and different. They don't judge the writer. They go with the flow. They can be the most powerful things in the world—forging signatures, signing contracts that could determine a lifetime of events, whether you pay your rent or not, whether you receive a letter or not. So important but yet so looked over. We don't pay attention to the small things in life. How things will go for us. The small things are what make the world wake up tomorrow.

I wrote this just after I moved to L.A. I had a hard time dealing with the pressure to always "be on" as I was finding my way in a new city.

EVERYONE IS...

haphazardly

aimlessly

hopelessly

searching

for

...something

everyone is

looking for something

better

bigger

richer

hotter

sweeter

everyone is

wishing they were someone else

wishing it was their turn

wondering why me

wishing they didn't have to do laundry

exercise

pretend

hold out for something more

wait

wait

...wait

everyone is

waiting for the next big thing
to realize a dream
to get a break
to prove them wrong

everyone is

secretly wishing at times
...they were anywhere but here

Shannon Johnson, mentor

This was taken from an exercise in my weekly writing meetings with my mentee, Melanie. We both wrote stories about dogs.

HEALING POWER OF THE MOON

Howling at the full moon, his voice was heard across the neighborhood. "You sound so sad, dear dog, What is the matter with you?"

"I am not sad, I am happy," he said. "I am celebrating the moon. It is a beacon on dark nights." I hadn't really thought of the moon being a beacon, but in a weird way, it sort of made sense to me.

The next night the moon was not full—it was hiding behind the thick, dark clouds. I didn't hear the sound of the dog howling. As I drove to the market, I had the weird feeling something was about to happen. Just as I was turning the corner, I hit something hard. I jumped out of the car and was shocked to see the dog laying in my path. Blood everywhere, his whimpers were barely audible above the strong wind. "Oh, no," I cried. "We must get you help, but where should I take you?"

"Let the moon be your beacon," whispered the dog. At that moment, I looked up into the sky and the clouds parted to expose the moon. "Follow it," he moaned.

I carefully lifted the dog into my car and followed the path of the big, bright moon. Just as I was about to lose hope, we came across an old Indian standing in an empty field. He beckoned me with his hands and as I pulled up, he reached into the car and grabbed the dog. As he cradled the dog in his arms, the Indian began chanting, staring all the while at the moon. Suddenly, the dog began howling and jumped out of the man's arms. The howling grew louder and the moon grew brighter. The dog was healed and the Indian smiled.

"Never underestimate the power of the moon," the Indian said as he smiled at me. "It has great power and is a beacon on dark nights."

Melissa Carolus Verlet, mentor

I wrote this piece in the Santa Cruz Mountains and reflected on the importance of life, not as it stands for one individual, but on the legacy we leave behind. It is the "ring" we create that determines our legacy.

THE FAIRY RING

From one tree, seemingly dead, stems many others.

This is like life. This is like my life.

The fairy ring isn't a stump with many living trees around it. It is, instead, a chance for one organism to give new hope to many others.

Perhaps, if I am so lucky, my time as a teacher will be like the old stump in the middle of a ring of new trees. Perhaps from all I have taught my students about things old—ancient, ancient peoples and places—will spring many smaller, younger, newer trees. Maybe once I am gone, what I have taught will remain. Maybe one tree will spring from the side, then another from above.

Perhaps, if I am very, very lucky, I will even spring life from within my hollow center, and she will grow up with an appreciation for all that is older but with a courage to continue to grow long after I am hollow, and ancient.

Like these trees.

Abby Kohn, mentor

I wrote this piece in the Poetry Workshop, which was great fun for me since the last time I wrote poetry, I was fifteen and a disgruntled adolescent. I read this piece at a WriteGirl reading because, in all honesty, my mentee, Mara, insisted that I read something, and she would not take no for an answer. And I'm glad I did.

I HATE IT WHEN PEOPLE SAY "I'M NOT RELIGIOUS, I'M SPIRITUAL," BUT...

The Buddha has been following me lately

At first, I think he was trying to find me through

Poseur ex-boyfriends with their pseudo-spirituality and their posters of the Dalai Lama.

Through neo-buddhist vegan and raw foodist, sometimes friends,

Through incense at bookstores and in self-help sections.

But now, the Buddha has gotten serious.

See, I dumped the college boyfriend with the Indian tapestries on his wall.

And the one with meaningful Japanese characters tattooed on his back (for real).

I have moved on from most of those crunchy, latent hippie friends.

And so the Buddha has had to get crafty.

He made a change—or I did—

He started to make sense.

(It is amazing where you go when the need is need.

It is amazing what you believe when the alternative is nothing.)

And so this Buddha, who was always hiding around my shadows

Lurking in those dingy apartments that smelled like amber and weed

Has begun moving in.

It started in the worst times.

He'd only come when I would listen to Joni Mitchell with purpose,

Lighting a candle on the deck, closing my eyes, looking for him.

Or anyone really.

But now he's bold

Sitting next to me in the car

Bouncing along beside me on a walk.

He's funny sometimes

So I let him in.

I think he's worried though

And me

That when the need goes

so will he.

Portia Frazier, age 14

I wrote this in my bedroom one night about my fear of the dark.

SONG OF FEAR

It roams through your body with every pitiful pumping
of your heart.
making its silent retreat
through your betraying blood.
creeping until your breath hitches,
and pain permeates the air you breathe.

Overtaking your senses and leaving its empty husk.
The fear that returns with the coming of every dusk.

Victoria Shao, age 17

Last spring, I cut and donated my hair to a charitable organization that makes wigs for children suffering from medical hair loss. Around the same time, my voice teacher died.

LOCKS OF LOVE

A bundle of my hair,
Thirteen inches worth, chopped off and tied up.
A much lighter head,
Me giggling, an ear-to-ear smile.
My hair, on its way to sharing that smile
With children lacking hair.

I feel good, knowing I have touched others.
When I've done well at a lesson,
When words of encouragement and praise shower me,
I float in a pool of her kind words.
A bubble of confidence within me, grows,
Until it bursts as a smile upon my face,
The perfect melody escapes.

Wrapped up safe in the warm blanket of her love.
Her beautiful voice and gentle advice
Continue to ring in my ears.

My world has been shattered, broken, lost.
I will never sing with her again.
My heart will never fill
With excitement, love and pride in quite the same way
Ever again. For, you see, she is gone.
A beloved teacher and friend, passed
Forever.

And yet, she remains with me in spirit, her presence
Always prodding me onward.
She believes in me, never lost faith, and never will.

Seasons have changed, now it is winter,
Other children wear my hair upon their heads.
Having hair, just like everyone else
Helps to coax their hearts into believing
They can soar high above the prison of discrimination.
With the help of my hair,
Their hearts are free to dream.

And in those same months
I have found my voice again.
I sing so loud that the heavens can hear.

Sakara El, age 17

I wrote this after the Heroine's Journey Workshop. I was learning to play with synesthesia.

LET'S RUN AWAY

Let's run away

Roaring in my ear

Like a monster

Ready

To attack

The thought of staying

Made me woozy

The thought of leaving made my heart race

Let's run away

Taste the rush of water

Feel the sound of bliss

Not knowing if I'd be happier gone

But ready to leave

Dissatisfied with everything around me

Should I settle for less? An old cliché

Echoing behind my roaring monster

There could be something

Exotic, innovative and full of passion out there for me

The final answer

Sweet monster of mine

I'm packed

Let's leave

Keren Taylor, mentor

I read a lot of folk tales as a child, staying up way past my bedtime, reading under the covers with a flashlight. The black and white of good and evil is so wonderfully clear, and as scary as they are, they can also be very comforting in their power. At WriteGirl we are always investigating our own culture, and writing this poem showed me how much Ukrainian folk tales are in my blood.

A SIMPLE FOLK TALE

Bite me, Baba Yaga

for I can sort grains of salt from sand

stay awake all night

spit fire

come back from I Know Not Where with I Know Not What,

find the 3 stone flowers

7 golden fishes

13 apples of youth

1000 nights

and a white duck.

Oh, I am Arabian too,

and descended from Vasilia the Wise.

You can't hide from me on your chicken legs

or lure me with a little round bun.

I've even set the wolf, the fox and the cock on each other.

They'll be dead by dawn.

Under the full moon, my white fur muff warms

cool porcelain hands,

and when I kick my red spike heels

I make bad mothers melt

into wax puddles.

Bad, ugly mothers should be cut out of all pages

and pasted to the side of butcher's trucks

so when you eat bloody meat,

remember the Cruella

who hides in your closet

and give her a big kiss

before opening the oven door,

whispering a gnarled curse

and throwing her in.

City of

Some
Angels

LOS ANGELES

I like how there always seems to be something going on. It's impossible to be bored in Los Angeles.

The incredible, eclectic mix of people in our city is what keeps me here despite the chaos. There are so many stories here.

Sometimes, the teenage mind just drifts. That's why we can be either ecstatic at one point and downright solemn at another.

JUST FOR TODAY

Friday nights are reserved for flying, sighing; my stream of consciousness thriving because my homework's piled high in the corner and all I can do for today is kiss Friday goodbye. Fantasizing of Melrose Avenue, up and down this eclectic metropolis, and I dream of you, my soon-to-be little pink iPod, dancing in the sky. You'll play Jimi Hendrix and I'll hum along because I don't quite know all the lyrics to "Purple Haze," but then again that's what everybody else does these days—pretend to know. And for today I'll be part of a statistic because it's tough to play the "nonconformist" when everyone else assumes the role. I won't let anyone find out that I listened to *NSYNC because I'll stay chained in my room, yes that's what I'll do. But part of me succumbs, and today I want to go shopping at the Buffalo Exchange. Oh how I'd love to live there and sleep in the dressing rooms and frolic through the musty vintage frocks... away from SATs and Queen Bee wannabes... it must be the Ventura Boulevard that Tom Petty sings about in his songs. What to do, when the weekend starts to kill you and you're stranded at home. I always come back to solitude, my favorite 'tude, and for today I'll settle for Jimi, and only Jimi, so "'scuse me while I kiss the sky."

During a mentoring session with my mentee, Lily, we were both a little tired and blocked. After talking about running the L.A. Marathon, it seemed natural to start writing about what it felt like to run it.

MARATHON DAY

They say never do anything new on the day of the marathon. On March 3, 2000, at 6 a.m., I arrived in downtown L.A. in my T-shirt and shorts, already shaking from the forty-five degree weather and outright fear. In addition to worrying about keeping my spirits up and my breakfast down, I now had to search for a trash bag to wear over my gear because it was raining. Hard. In the fifteen years the marathon had been held, they had never seen weather like this on race day. I wasn't sure if the city had seen weather like this—ever. We finally took our marks. The gunshot signaled the start, and we were off! And, as if on cue, the heavens opened. It wasn't just raining—it was a monsoon. It was biblical. Lightning sizzled overhead, hail—HAIL—smacked the pavement, drowning out the sound of runners' feet slogging through puddles. As I pondered the soaked mess that were my socks and shoes, I wondered if I should take this as a sign from above. God himself did not want me to race, and he was going to quite a bit of trouble to communicate this.

One of the most clichéd but reliable philosophies regarding Los Angeles is that it is a depository for people who need to be admired. Not surprisingly, the L.A. Marathon is not marketed as the fastest course or having the most coveted prize but as the RACE WITH A MILLION SPECTATORS. That's approximately 38,000 fans per mile to ogle your every fabulous, aching step. There are also around fifteen bands to help keep your mind off the grueling task at hand, so for the runner in love with spectacle and distraction, this race sounded ideal. There were not a million spectators that day. I'm not sure if there were even a few thousand. But, amazingly, there was someone on every street corner, shivering and braving the rain to cheer us on. Wet, bedraggled and wearing a trash bag poncho, I could hardly believe that these strangers were telling me I was amazing. That I could do it. That I was almost there. It was the day I fell hard for Los Angeles. It's also the reason the L.A. Marathon is the best-kept secret holiday of the year. Angelenos do not often make eye contact, or say "bless you" when you sneeze, or hold open doors, or return a smile. But on marathon day, those same strangers were screaming my name and those of my soggy comrades, and they carried us home.

Amy Morton, mentor

I wrote some of this during the Poetry Workshop. I was facing a career change and felt excited and terrified. Palm trees are often seen simply as the emblem of paradise, but they're always weathering change.

THE PALM TREE

The massive green-brown leaves sway and shake,

leaning left as if listening to a secret.

Palm trees in strong wind

are like lanky soldiers in a growing melee.

They fight to hold my world in place.

(Is there something in nature that makes us fear change?)

The constant rustling is kindling for my thoughts.

A smooth fire of clarity begins to burn

through the bland taste of routine,

the clinical overhead lights, the worn grey carpet,

the glaring monitor and the blinking phone.

I am reminded of my hopes, my wants, my needs.

My inner pilot light flickers with rebellion

as big as the cloudless sky I cannot see from my desk.

Change is sweeping through like the Santa Anas,

and I must hold the ground like the palm tree.

My head rustles but my planted feet hold on

To me.

Melanie Gonzalez, age 18

This piece came from an experiment during which my mentor, Shannon, and I wrote about what life would be like in the future.

CEREBRIA

There's a gigantic freeway network right above the city, but I live in the lake, where the water is green and thick. The sound of water beats against my ears like a million hearts. There are flashlight fish, and dead bodies sinking below. I can see what goes on beyond the surface if I get close enough, but no one sees me, because the water acts like a two-way mirror. Those who look into the water see themselves as monsters with grinning fangs from cheek to cheek.

Here it is always dark. People have learned to live in the sewer, and when they come up to the streets, they look like muddy swamp creatures. Everything is expensive. We must save the little money we have. To stay alive, we must wear gas masks that cover our entire face. Everyone knows who I am when they see me in my white uniform with the big red cross in front: the time recorder. Armed with my bag of spray cans and extra air supply, I record the days, and old stories. When I am done with the last passage, I sign my name, Cerebria, with big cryptic lime-green letters. If I don't, everyone will forget the old stories from back in the day. This is the importance of recording human existence.

As I walk, someone tries to be slick by snatching my bag. I grab the culprit's neck with my long tentacle hair. The split ends snip the flesh from his bones, and fling him onto a clothesline. To live here you have to think fast. Once, a man in a black trench coat tried to steal my recording wall. He tried to remove my gas mask to suffocate me, but I pushed him into his car and lit all his cigarettes. I watched him blow up as the smoke from the blast turned the sky into a red sunset.

Fear heightens all five senses. Sometimes I find myself like a cat with its fur standing on end, my spine shivering as the wind kisses my back, causing me to jerk all of a sudden, forcing me to look back, even though I am unsure of facing the new danger. I want to curl up in warmth, away from this world, but I must continue recording time.

Stephanie Almendarez, age 17

Early one morning, I observed a man digging in a trash can in front of my apartment. He picked out a can, shook it and drank its leftovers. That night, I wrote about what I would do if I had 24 hours to live. I decided I'd go to my long-lost love—it wouldn't matter if I died, because I'd lived that last day to my fullest. The title of the poem was taken from one of my favorite Red Hot Chili Peppers songs called "Dosed."

TAKE IT AWAY, I NEVER HAD IT ANYWAY

It is sunrise.

I might die tomorrow, you know. At midnight. I'm not sure yet.

Not friend, she's material—
This City of no sunny Angels.
Soul, why don't I throw her away?
She's rare and perfectly fed,
Especially now with her extreme fake-over.
But she's not painted yellow-brick gold.

It's noon now. Winking at me in her yearning, the soda can speaks to me.
I shake her up, what's left; drink her down.

I stand at the peak of Elysian Park, overlooking the tired city.
My dog sits silently in my cart. She's real jealous.

Maybe I'll taste the mountains, the train-tracks, maybe the trees.
Because tomorrow I might be gone.
My soul could go to the sky.
But maybe I'll be a cloud.

I'm going home now.
To the woman I've always loved.
Hope she accepts me.

I might die tomorrow, you know. At midnight. I'm not sure yet.

It's sundown.

Hilary Galanoy, mentor

I usually write comedy, so it was fun to write something more serious. And just like when writing comedy, a serious essay still requires a certain rhythm to the words.

VIEW OUT MY KITCHEN WINDOW

Sometimes I like to stand at my kitchen window and look out; maybe I'm sipping coffee (nonfat creamer and Sweet 'N Low) or even eating breakfast over the sink (English muffin, yogurt, a fresh orange). There's not that much to see—my rain gutter, the neighbor's pitched roof, the backyard tree branches (all-season verdant) swaying into frame. Mostly, the view is sky. Sometimes crystal clear. Not so much lately. Sometimes it's lady finger clouds, elegantly spaced, like some fancy bakery dessert. Sometimes the clouds are big and angry and fluffy and bruised like a bulldog's face. Other times, the sky is dull, flat grey, the static snow of a TV screen. You lose focus watching; fade away. Idly waiting for the raindrops to start falling. Then the water gushes out of the rain spout, splashing onto my unseen front steps, giving the stark view a new age soundtrack. And then some mornings, it's just perfect. Warm blue, faded around the edges, like a mothy old vintage dress you find in the back of Goodwill. I'll open up the window and let the outside in, the traffic, the air, the sun. I smile and start the dishes.

Buildings, design and architecture affect us on many different levels.

PANORAMA

Glimpses of that sad, off-white, worn-down building
Fifty stories high,
Dirty looking walls
With striking angles
Window after window stacked on top
Of one another
Every day my eyes meet this fancy structure of architecture
Historical landmark, County General Hospital
Stands tall, surrounded by homes like mine
I was taken there as a child with the flu or fever
I last saw my mother alive in the ICU
My only visits to this part of town were sad sickly moments
I'm back in this city, my home stands parallel to the
Hospital, an emblem of bittersweet memories

Irene Daniel, mentor

One winter evening, I was sitting in my backyard watching the sun go down. I just closed my eyes and listened as the day turned to night. This stream-of-consciousness writing is the result of all of my experiences in WriteGirl, where I've learned how much I can sense and feel when I am still.

VESPERS IN THE NEIGHBORHOOD

I hear the freeway rumble

I watch the light grow dim

In my garden

A dog barks

A car horn honks

Pots and pans clang

A simmering supper

Scents the air

These are the evening prayers

Of the city

As twilight

Takes the day

My former mentee and I were working on how to write about a secret. It's refreshing to confess, but it's much easier and more enjoyable to write it than to tell someone.

CITRUS THIEVES

The night air is getting colder. I can tell because the cats are beginning to sleep on the bed again. The underground furnace has burned off its summer dust. And I find myself putting on socks in the morning. It's autumn here in Los Angeles and I can't wait for the winter.

Not only do the rains clear out the smoggy air, showing off the Southland's sparkling ocean and verdant hills, but the winter chill welcomes the citrus season. Ripe fruits of vermillion and yellows hang invitingly from their weighted limbs. Even now, my mouth puckers from the thought of warm lemon cakes and waking up to freshly squeezed orange juice.

We have a young lemon tree of our own, already boasting green fruits with promises of yellow treasures in a few weeks. But that lonely tree's harvest is hardly enough to satisfy my appetite for citrus. So, my husband and I have taken to late-night foraging around the neighborhood.

Our nighttime walks didn't begin with stealthy purposes. They began innocently like so many bad habits. We would meander through the streets, visiting friendly felines, walking past quiet homes and listening to muffled voices emanating with the soft light from curtained windows.

It all started with one orange, waiting invitingly from an overhanging branch. I was only tempted at first. Trying to ignore the bright color shining in the moonlight. The second night was more than I could handle.

So satisfying was my hand around that oily skin that I began peeling the fruit right then and there. It was juicy and cold, naturally refrigerated by the night air. Discarding the peel, my hands were so sticky, I had to wash them in someone's sprinklers. But by then, I was already hooked.

My husband and I would purposely wear coats with deep pockets to fill with our evening's gatherings. We became familiar with which trees bore the best treasures, which owners never bothered to harvest theirs and which ones were the easiest to grab.

Our guilt was quieted by the fruits that rotted and fell moldy to the ground, wasted by those who didn't appreciate their arborous gifts. We would reward ourselves with tangy treats, fragrant and flavored by the freshly picked fruits.

As I put on my socks this morning I breathe in the crisp air. The cold reminds me there is a lemon tree waiting for me up the hill. Now all I have to do is find that lemon tart recipe I've saved in a drawer somewhere.

In this piece, I recall a night spent with my friends at a concert. I wanted the reader to get a sense of the kind of environment I was in, and at the same time, know my opinions about the people and things I saw.

THE SEARCH

I went to a concert at the Troubadour in Hollywood with two of my friends on Saturday night. We've been to concerts like these and have always hoped we'd meet a guy. Well, we've never had much luck. The scene is always a dark, crowded room with horrible singers on stage belting out the note they think rocks. Meanwhile, the boys are pushing and shoving each other in the mosh pit—an area which isn't really defined, and therefore you'll hear girls screaming once in a while from what the boys think is a harmless shove. I look around at the girls dressed in their slutty, wannabe-punk outfits, dancing crazily and acting like true fans of the music. I'm annoyed by them, but jealous at the same time, because they're the ones meeting the boys.

Sometimes I really wonder whether I need to wear revealing outfits or an excessive amount of makeup for a guy to pay an ounce of attention to me. You think you look "hot" in your new jeans and T-shirt, only to feel disappointed when you see girls in their new mini-skirts and low-cut tops. I mean, what kind of world do we live in anyway, and are guys really that shallow? Anyway, I know I cannot begin to dress that way, especially because I want a guy to like me for me. But will it ever end, this search for one guy with whom I can actually have a relationship?

When we arrive at the Troubadour, we wait outside in a long line behind two teenage girls in their vintage-style outfits smoking cigarettes. I hug myself while my teeth chatter from the cold. I guess my parents are right about not leaving the house without a jacket. But I was definitely not going to wear a ski jacket again, like that time at Disneyland. How embarrassing.

We finally buy the tickets and walk into the dark room; the only lights are those on stage with the bands playing. The boys on stage look like middle-schoolers. "Great," I say sarcastically to myself. "I'm going to be surrounded by these immature boys the entire night." I lift my shoulders and turn sideways to squeeze myself between the crowds of people. I hold my breath to escape that awful b.o. smell as my arms rub against the sweaty backs of those tall teen boys. My friends and I finally make it to the other side of the room where there's space to walk around and breathe. I listen to the band, the guitarist with his squeaky voice begging the booing audience for one more song. As irritated as I am with their endless performance, I actually feel bad for him. No matter what people's opinions are, it is always disrespectful to let them know through mockery. "Get off the stage! Boo! You suck!" What an embarrassment.

Zoe Beyer, age 16

I thought about what it would be like if something crazy, like cracking seashells, could change things in the world. It's a pretty absurd idea, but it is something I think about sometimes. When I write poems, I like to create situations and realities that don't quite exist in real life, but are not that far-fetched. Finding a dried mussel won't make the sun come up, of course, but in poetry these ideas can exist.

GLASS

And if we cracked seashells at dawn we would be better people.
We would look into ourselves, about ourselves, under our
Fingernails and broken body parts for that missing
Shard of conch or cerith.
And if you found that dried mussel under your white bed sheet,
The sun would come up over our dead city.
Like the time my grandmother sliced her foot on a piece of sea glass,
We will bleed into the ocean and the sand and the salt will sting.

Soles of

Our Shoes

TRAVELING

The Karakorem Mountains in Pakistan
are what my name comes from.
Someday I'll go there.

Janine M. Coughlin, mentor

I wrote this during Cecilia's travel writing segment at the Creative Nonfiction Workshop. When I first wrote the piece, it was focused on the crazy time I had trying to get from Canada to South Carolina to see my friend in the middle of a business trip. When I sat down to edit it, the focus shifted to my trying to impress my friend's daughter and falling flat on my face in the process.

KODAK LOBSTER MOMENTS

I'm eager to get out of Halifax before the winter storm shuts the airport. I've managed to insert a twenty-hour layover in Charleston, South Carolina into a ten-day, five-city business trip that began in Calgary and ends in New Orleans. My childhood best friend, Lorraine, who I haven't seen in two years, lives in Charleston. She's glad I'll be stopping in, but needs a small favor. I have to pretend I know the Tooth Fairy.

Her daughter, Laura, has been pestering her for details about this fantastic being who started trading her quarters for bicuspids in the middle of the night. Weary of thinking up explanations for what the Tooth Fairy does with all the teeth, she told Laura I was friends with her, and suggested she ask me about her next time she saw me, assuming that wouldn't happen for months.

I'm in the Halifax airport trying to imagine what the Tooth Fairy does with all the teeth when I see the lobsters. One of my favorite childhood photos is of me and my brother—I'm six, he's two—and with a mixture of effort, wonder and excitement, we are hoisting a pair of lobsters out of a cardboard box on the kitchen floor. So when I see that tank, I think, it's not enough to tell Laura I hang out with the Tooth Fairy. No, to cement my "cool" factor, I'll buy Laura her own Kodak lobster moment.

The flight takes off late and as we near the Toronto airport, I'm panicking. I've only got 20 minutes to get to the Delta terminal on the opposite side of the airport and board the last flight to Atlanta. The minute the plane touches down, I grab the lobsters in their cardboard carry on and run. I make it out of the terminal just as the shuttle bus pulls away. With the crazed urgency of a contestant on The Amazing Race, I see a woman dropping off her elderly mother and beg her to drive me and the lobsters around to the Delta terminal on her way out of the airport.

Miraculously, the lobsters and I make the Atlanta flight. However, due to "mechanical difficulties," the flight from Atlanta is delayed and it's 4 a.m. when the lobsters and I finally arrive in Charleston. Lorraine is there to meet us. We tuck the lobsters into her fridge as the sun rises, and Lorraine confides that she doesn't actually like lobsters. I don't mind, sure that Laura will.

When I wake up, Laura asks me if I really know the Tooth Fairy. I say yes and she runs away giggling. Just before I leave, the lobsters are unveiled. I make Lorraine take out her camera. But instead of reacting with excitement and wonder, Laura peers into the box and runs screaming with terror from the room. She's still teary when she hugs me goodbye, but I get a tiny smile when I say I'll give the Tooth Fairy a big hello for her.

I traveled through Romania and wrote this on a train.

EVERYTHING'S A PHOTO OP

boy in blue track suit
endless uneven rows of lopsided haystacks
like Stonehenge but not

a once blue once red train without windows
green worn doors on grey barns

the fat man at the station with what looks like
a flyswatter

horses pulling wagons
ducks sheep cows
cornfields ragged and dry
ravaged by deaf crows
ignoring the cries of the scarecrow
hanging his head and arms from a cross

with a scythe and a sideways surge
a slender man cuts tall grasses
in his underwear
summer heat in Moldavia banishes vanity

one bright blue door shouts
from a shack between silvery birch trees
a sudden deep breath from the stranger next to me
a hairy Romanian in a bold polyester sweater
air thick with man scent

metal on metal, screeching around corners
we find our true age
here on a slow train
in an old country

Katherine Taylor, mentor

This is an excerpt from a story I wrote after taking a cross-country road trip with my mother. The longer story is part of a collection to be published by HarperCollins in spring 2006.

TRAVELING WITH MOTHER

That summer, people in the Midwest were dying from the heat. I had never thought about the Midwest except as space on the map between California and New York. That summer, my brother ran an unmarked cop car off the road on the 99 between Stockton and Sacramento and was charged with assault with a deadly weapon. My grandmother was moved out of her house and into The Home. My obese Auntie Petra lost 75 pounds by having a shake for breakfast, a shake for lunch and a sensible dinner.

My hair came out in clumps. In New York I was worried and nervous and couldn't concentrate. I had moved there the previous autumn to act and write but found myself too homesick to do anything but cry and socialize. I threw enormous parties to make myself feel less lonesome and my neighbors left nasty notes threatening to tear me asunder. A man wearing rollerblades molested me on 68th street. I had the screens removed from my windows in case I decided to jump out. Instead, I decided to fly home to California.

In Los Angeles I called my hairdresser. His name is Armando and I roll the "R." I said, "I don't care how busy you are. I have an emergency. My hair is falling out." He said, "First you come, we cut it all off. Then you stop worrying about whatever you worry." He rolls his R's too. Armando knows all my secrets.

In Los Angeles I met with a producer who had written a part for me in a film financed by rich Germans. I told him, "I'm not an actress anymore. I won't prostitute my emotions." Afterwards, I felt ridiculous. Afterwards, I wondered why I seemed to have no control over the things that came out of my mouth.

The dog died the day I arrived at my parents' house in Fresno. The bionic dog, the three thousand dollar chemotherapy dog. Cancer ate his ears off. Daddy Taylor had brought that mutt dog home after he ran over my dalmatian with his truck on my tenth birthday. My brothers and I had marked the dalmatian's grave in the backyard with a cross and stones. After the mutt dog died of cancer, I suggested we bury it in the pet cemetery outside. Daddy said, "What cemetery?"

I said, "Where you buried Buttons after you smashed her."

He said, "Katherine, I scraped that dog off the driveway and threw it in the garbage."

I said, "That's against sanitation laws."

My mother agreed. She got wild-eyed and said, "Your father yells at me when I break the speed limit."

This is an excerpt from my travel log from a trip to Costa Rica.

PURA VIDA ADVENTURES

After nearly ten hours of traveling and twenty minutes at Customs, we've finally arrived. The moistness of the humidity hits me immediately, and the warmth of the sun beats on my tired body. Not even ten minutes later, I begin to sweat. Erik and I have finally arrived in Costa Rica—the start of our first vacation in Central America and our first vacation together.

Slowly moving towards the hotel, I begin to notice my surroundings. The smell of rain lingers in the air and the lush green of the rainforest is everywhere. I can almost taste the sweetness of the country, while the sounds of a foreign language ring in my ears. Eager to explore (with my guidebook's suggestions already flagged), a wave of tiredness and hunger washes over me. Erik and I decide to leave our luggage in our room and spend the evening enjoying our first "Tican" meal of rice, black beans and fresh fish.

The next day, after a cup of fresh Costa Rican coffee, I'm ready to explore the beach and the Manuel Antonio National Park. Famed for its beauty and wildlife, Erik was looking forward to seeing some monkeys and sloths, while I was excited to mark the park off my "1,000 Places to See Before You Die" list. We decide to take the local bus from our hotel to the park. Even thought the drive was just downhill, my head starts to spin and my stomach aches. When we step off the bus, I immediately realize something is wrong. I turn to Erik and notice that his face is pale as well. Hours later, we emerge from the local restaurant's bathroom only to realize that we have food poisoning. I guess that fresh fish wasn't so fresh after all.

Rayline Rivera, age 14

I wrote this story during the travel writing section of the Creative Nonfiction Workshop. As I remembered more details, the story became more interesting to write.

HOME

One day I was walking home from my friend's house. I had just moved to the city so I wasn't familiar with it. It started to get dark and I couldn't see anything because there were no street lights anywhere to be found. It was so dark everywhere and I kept trying to read each street sign to find mine. I couldn't find it anywhere. I kept telling myself "I'm not lost" but I was. It was so cold and foggy, which made it even harder to find my way home. My stomach was all tied into a knot and I wanted to cry so bad. No one was out for me to ask for directions, so I knew I was in trouble. I sat down on a curb under a tree, feeling hopeless. I was mostly worried about my mom. The way she would feel about my not getting home on time and thinking all these horrible thoughts about what had probably happened to me. I was so scared and cold, wondering if I would ever get home.

As I was sitting down on the curb with my head in my lap, I heard my mother calling and saying "Rayline, come inside for dinner." As I picked my head up, I saw her across the street standing on the porch. I ran as quickly as possible to reach her, I jumped on her and gave her a huge hug as if it had been forever since I had last seen her. I could tell that she felt all weird about it because I didn't let her go. We sat down at our kitchen table. Eating dinner, I told my family about my whole situation and about how I felt. They were all surprised because I had never done anything this silly before. So next time I plan to go to a friend's house, I'll make sure I find a ride home.

Janine M. Coughlin, mentor

I wrote this in a writing class—the exercise was about coming up with a location that was as specific as possible. I was driving back to L.A. from Death Valley, and drove through this scary little town called Troma, which is the setting for the story.

WELCOME TO TROMA

The angry red warning light had been on for about ten minutes before Melody Jones realized she was nearly out of gas. She squinted out the windshield at the desolate highway, which seemed to stretch off into the horizon like a long grey carpet. She thought she saw the spires of a church poking up just over the hills, and hoped that meant civilization was waiting for her ahead.

A few more miles and she saw an exit sign. She turned off and found herself in Troma, population 594, elevation 3,000 feet. She blinked and she was on Main Street—nothing more than a cluster of buildings in front of a borax mine that left the land looking more like a location for a sci-fi film set on a distant planet. It seemed Trauma would have been a better name for the town. Blinking again, she found herself in front of GUS'S GAS & GRUB SHAK.

Melody pulled in and wished she had a gun in her purse, or at least one of those Swiss army knife keychains. All she had was a nail clipper and a pack of gum. She surveyed the "Grub Shak"—a windowless block of concrete with a big can of Budweiser hand-painted on the side. Great, she thought. There's no self-service. I'm gonna have to go into the Grub Shak and I probably won't come out alive.

She got out of her car, making a fist with her keys in her hand so that the keys poked out between each of her fingers, something she remembered reading about in a magazine article on self-defense for women. Slowly she pushed open the door of the Shak. The room was silent. The only light seemed to be coming from a few vending machines lined up against the wall to her left. There was a long bar at the back of the room, with a Buddha-like statue next to the cash register.

Suddenly the statue spoke to her.

"What can I do for you little lady?" asked the statue, which she realized, as the statue hopped off the bar, was really a man the size of a midget. Well, he really was a midget.

Melody was so startled she dropped her keys. "Um, I need some gas please."

"Sure," said the man. "I'm Gus, by the way. Where you coming from?"

"Death Valley," Melody said.

"And where you headed?" Gus asked.

"Edwards," she answered. "The Air Force Base."

Something big doesn't have to happen for you to write about a place you've been and what you experienced while you were there.

THE FRINGE

Cobblestone, fish and chips and kilts with knee socks on men. It was one of the best months of my life. I rollerbladed down tree-lined streets and up hills that led to our flat. Performed in a pub where the beers were as dark as my hair. Wore a jean jacket that was left in the flat by a Scotsman or Scotsgirl. Walked through the park being serenaded by a group of kids about Madonna and Michael Jackson, to the tune of "The Star Spangled Banner." Found the only restaurant in town that had vegetables and became a regular. Lived with six other comedians in two rooms, making for some very unfunny fights. Found a favorite cookie with jam and stuck to it. Got good at darts and showering fast. Visited Loch Ness in the rain and watched my friend fall in love with a girl he just met. Took lots of pictures of them and had endless conversations about the probability of her writing him. Made the amount of my paycheck in long-distance phone calls. Stared at my boyfriend's picture and dreamed of being back home. Finally got home and dreamed of when I'd return.

Susan Abram, mentor

I wrote this at the Creative Nonfiction Workshop when we were writing about traveling. It was inspired by a cross-country road trip to Los Angeles with my nutty friend.

TUMBLING DOWN

Somewhere in Texas on the 10 West, my best friend in the whole world is evaporating.

She is the driver. I am the passenger. We are in the middle, between New York and Los Angeles, between dream and reality, between flesh and ash.

We are tumbleweed.

Texas on the 10 West will do that to you.

It will make you forget the stories she told you of travel, like lullabies of freedom that made your mouth water, and led you away from home in the first place.

It will make you erase the future you imagined, the pink stuccoed apartment with a courtyard that you will rent once you get to Hollywood.

It will make you long for the last town you left behind, where the gas station attendants called you ma'am and tried to guess your country of origin because it doesn't make any sense to them that a woman with hair so black it's blue, and coffee-colored eyes and skin toasted by the sun... could be from where they live.

All that vanishes on the 10 West, where you begin to count the carcasses of armadillo.

"Are you dry?" I ask her.

She rubs her freckled arms.

"Yeah, I'm dry."

I hold up a glass of water for her to drink.

"Oh... you mean that kind of dry."

We laugh for a moment. Only a moment. Texas on the 10 West is too serious for us. It is a funeral compared to New Orleans, where jazz and blues oozed from opened doors as we drove under canopies of century-old cypress and magnolia trees where rusted Mardi Gras beads still dangled.

She drinks from the glass like a fish stranded on land, whose lips barely reach the edge of a pond.

"Still thirsty?" I ask.

"No," she says. "I don't know what I am."

"Me neither," I say.

We count Ford and Chevy pick-ups that pass us. We try to guess what animal the rifles that are pinned to the racks of the truck beds were pointed at.

Two days driving through the Lone Star State in my silver Honda Civic packed with everything I own outright, and we feel like we have been stranded in space.

Houston, we have a problem.

A sign down the road reads "Las Cruces," "The Crossroads" ...New Mexico.

"Yay!!!" I say, as if I am ten years old, rather than 31.

"We're almost in Los Angeles, Sweetie!" she says.

We are quiet again as I begin to imagine my pink stuccoed apartment with the courtyard and Spanish mission-style terracotta tiles and water fountain, and the new friends I'll make who will come over for dinner parties, and...

Then I remember. We are still in Texas, on the 10 West, miles away from Los Angeles, a city named after angels which some say exist and others say do not, and then it hits me... We are still far from Earth.

Thinking about all the places I've been, I've come to believe that everyone should have their own pair of traveling boots.

WAITING

Grim, mature-looking construction boots have accompanied my every endeavor the last few years.

Road trip to Mexico City in 2001 to climb the Teotihuacan pyramids. Along they came to D.C. for half a year as a student. In 2003, visiting my grandfather's childhood village, learning about the strong Arab influence in that secluded town hidden between mountainous regions of Jalisco. They trotted to the Yucatan peninsula by the Caribbean contemplating the cross of the Belizean/Mexican border. Walked the rich, plush soil of many territories.

My rugged boots with creases, dirt, stains are hibernating in my closet and waiting for the adventures laying ahead of them.

*Set your story in the middle
of the Indian Ocean,
on top of a petunia or
in the cellar after a flood.*

REMINISCING

In
Retrospect

I remembered something insignificant, but sweet.

Erica Drennan, age 15

I originally wrote this as a story. It really wasn't working out, so I tried writing it as a poem instead, which was new for me. I was able to put most of the lines into meter without them seeming forced. Poetry isn't quite as hard as I thought.

fuzzy sweet

summer evenings on the porch
underneath the freckled sky
catching fireflies in our hands
"fairy pet," you used to say
peaches picked from wispy trees
can you taste the fuzzy sweet?

'member, too, those orchard skies
dreamed our trees were palace keeps
you were king and I was queen
ruling subjects in the night
crickets, tree frogs, nightingales
orchestra we hired for court.

now subjects do not pay their tax
kingdom's falling all apart
music's stopped, the players left
waiting here, I watch the sky
hoping for just one more chance
summer evenings on the porch.

Dana Valenzuela, mentor

This piece originated from a recent trip to a place I once called home.

THE RETURN

The house sits tall and is shaped like it gave birth to another. The familiar objects hung about decorate the modest interior. Photos hung next to figurines that were once in the other home. I notice some items are missing. Furniture carefully positioned as if not moved from the late nineties. She makes her home by positioning the things that make her comfortable. The furniture, the photos, the figurines; so many memories found in the things.

I sense the missing. The memories burn a hole in my heart. It hurts to remember and see these objects here. Next to the furniture, the photos and the figurines, there was once a life.

I half expect him to come in and check on me the way he used to. I repeat the cliché, if I would have known then that I'd only have a few more "check ins" left in my lifetime with him, I might have paused and engaged him with more words than, "I'm fine Dad."

I might have more memories of him, of those times, of those moments. But for now, I notice how she's going about the grief and the life without him. I watch in stillness without any other observations because I know that the missing is always present.

I fell in love with Sandra Cisneros's House on Mango Street and read it over and over. I decided I'd try her style to write about my experiences at the house on 51st Street.

PARTY ON 51st STREET

The house on 51st Street was a two-story wooden house, bluish-gray on the outside, with white walls and wooden floors on the inside. There were five legal rooms in this house— two on the first floor and three on the top. There were two more rooms that my dad later annexed.

Outside in the front yard, my mom planted roses at the edges of the garden, near the soon-to-be fence. I can distinctly remember the smell of pink and red roses mixed with the fertilizer she'd buy at Home Base. I loved it. It smelled funny, but also like home.

Loud parties were always happening. The house on 51st Street was vibrant and teeming with people. A party would be thought up a month before the date. A week before, the guests would be invited. A day before, the grill would be cleaned.

The day of the party, we'd all wake up early in the morning to start the preparations. My mom mopped the floors up and down the living room, dining room, kitchen and hallways. The guys upstairs, my uncles, vacuumed and threw out their own trash. We, the little kids, my brother, sister and I, were in charge of getting dirty outside—playing till my mom finished her chores and had time to bathe and change us into our *estrenos,* our new clothing.

The yellow kitchen was bright with my mom's presence. The oven itself smelled like a bakery. It contained rows of *pansitos.* They were white and soft on the inside, and toasty brown on the outside. My mom made all kinds of salads on the cutting board. On top of the stove boiled eggs for the potato salad. The smell of warm mayonnaise, mustard, potatoes, celery and eggs was delicious. It was almost angelic.

The music went hand in hand with the food. My mom was always the DJ, playing records of Eddie Santiago, Juan Luis Guerra and, occasionally, some English love songs. I remember, one night at a party, during a certain song of Juan Luis Guerra's—"Quisiera Ser un Pes"—I stood behind the big Victorian sofa in the living room, with a feeling brought out in me—inexplicable. I was peeking, through my little girl eyes, at the many couples slow-dancing to this beautiful song. I didn't know what the song was saying, but the rhythm of the dancers went hand in hand with the flow. I also remember not seeing my parents dancing together, like the many beautiful couples. My mom, with her frizzy hair, was recording the moment with the huge video-camera on her shoulder, and my dad was standing at the doorway, Budweiser in hand, looking out, past the porch, at God knows what.

The house on 51st Street is gone now, vanished. Only a picture remains. Just a few years ago, it was sold to the Boys & Girls Club—they tore it down to make space for a parking lot.

Ariana Horwitz, age 14

Writing helps me through the rough times. When I discovered that my friend was having the same troubles I was going through, writing about hers helped me understand both of us better.

MEMORIES

I take the long road to nowhere
Hoping it will someday take me somewhere.
Bumblebees buzz in the trees
Making me honey that's as sweet as can be.
Disappearing in the grass, tall
I wish these small moments would always last.

Making memories with my friends
We will travel together till the end of time
No matter how hard our paths get
We will find a way to get by
And come together when our love is gone
Not wander off until it's back where it belongs
These are the memories I cherish most

Stormy skies, eyes filled with lies
I can hear your cry calling me near
I conquer my fear just to reach you
We live on adventure and run into battles
We have broken free
And we will make the best
Memories.

Jayna Rust, mentor

After I went to the Poetry Workshop, I went home to spend time in my small hometown. I had to write about the snow.

SMALL-TOWN SNOW

I open my eyes and
snow spits across the windshield.
Scared, I scan the roads—
So long since I've been in snow or sleet.
The highways are OK,
so I close my eyes again
somewhat comforted.

If it's going to be teeth-chattering, skin-drying cold,
At least I'll have snow.

Our snow is different here.
It smells like spring water—
not really anything, just pure, clean.

It is stunning coming down,
and it stays that way—untouched, uncorrupted.
Not like the snows of the city—
No sooner has the beauty entered the city than it's turned
to splashed-up brown sludge,
like everything else around it.

A mid-winter snow
One of the few nice things here.

At least I have snow.

Jennifer Repo, mentor

Music has always been a big influence in my life and I wanted to write about its companionship over the years.

AURAL REFLECTIONS

On a date, I usually like to ask, "What's in your CD player right now?" The answers vary, of course, but I'm usually satisfied. Thank God "Stryper" has never been an answer. Music tells a lot about someone. Yes, this might be judgmental or superficial, but c'mon. How many times have we sat across the table from someone scrutinizing how they eat or looking for signs that they treat their mother well?

I had a not-so-typical upbringing. Sure, I was fed, clothed, housed and nurtured, but in many ways, rock 'n' roll raised me. At age eleven, I found The Rolling Stones. While Mick Jagger lusted his way through "Gimme Shelter" and "Wild Horses," I stumbled through my first crushes. In fact, "Angie" played in the background while I shared my first kiss with Mike Benzy. Even as a young girl, I sensed the emotional drama that relationships could bring on even though I had yet to hold a boy's hand. The seductiveness of their lyrics and those red Stones lips beckoned me to leave Andy Gibb and Shawn Cassidy behind. I did, and never looked back.

I learned about community from the Grateful Dead. Their music is fun, though they're not exactly known for their definitive musicianship. With the loyalty of a honeybee, I went to shows whenever they played in California. This wasn't just about going to a concert. It was an experience. Parking lots transformed into homes for many of the permanently dedicated. Deadland, as it came to be known, was a thirty-year Summer of Love: hippies, patchouli oil, vegetarian egg rolls, drum circles, face painting, dancing, woven colored bracelets. Sitting down in the parking lot with people I'd just met, we talked, shared, laughed and communed over a common interest. School socialized me, taught me how to play well in the sandbox. But Dead shows taught me about humanity, about being free of judgment as Jerry sings: "Sunshine, daydream, walking in the tall trees, going where the wind goes."

"Say a prayer for the cowgirl her horse ran away," sings Emmylou Harris in "Ballad of a Runaway Horse." Never before had I been interested in country or bluegrass or anything remotely connected to the "cheatin,' hurtin' pick-up truck" style. Harris has always delved deeper than some of her contemporaries. But approaching my mid-twenties, I discovered her beautifully crafted harmonies. Here was a woman singing about the human condition. Most artists do to some extent, but Emmylou sings to the soul. The complicated woman's soul. And she was saying, it's okay to be complicated. I then realized that her lyrics were a direct reflection of my inner-life. All music that I've connected to, whether it be Metallica, The Dead or Sarah McLachlan, has lifted me up, talked to me, inspired me and affirmed that I was not alone. So I leave you with this question: What's in your CD player?

I got home from a date and couldn't believe I played video games!

ONE PLAYER

For someone who has always embraced technology, I'm sorely behind in one genre: video games.

When I moved to Los Angeles, I thought I'd try to find a job back in the interactive space. I quickly found out most West Coast agencies are attached to the gaming industry.

"Do you have any gaming experience?" a freshly pierced 20-something asked me in an interview.

I was too embarrassed to reply, "Why yes, Ms. Pac Man at the McLean, Virginia Pizza Hut in 1982."

My first exposure to video games was actually in 1977. My best friend was the first person on the block with Atari's Pong. It was the black and white Wimbledon of fake tennis games. After five minutes of playing, we'd get bored and go outside.

Twenty years later, I was working for an interactive development shop. One Friday, the guys asked me to be a player in a networked version of Quake. I didn't know the rules and I never earned the right weapons, so they slaughtered me. I got bored and went home 10 minutes later.

Recently, a date introduced me to Sony's PlayStation 2. I mentioned I was curious about the violence surrounding Grand Theft Auto. With the controller in hand, I learned to speed, run into trees and steal cop cars. I don't know what all the video game violence hype is about. Killing hookers with chain saws was fun.

After 15 minutes, my adult-onset ADD kicked in and I wanted to do something else, but it was too dark to go outside to play. We ate brownies and watched the Cartoon Network instead.

I've come a long way since Pong.

Cecilia Hae-Jin Lee, mentor

This is from the first chapter of "Yes, No, Thank You, Coca-Cola," the first in a trilogy of books I'm currently writing about my childhood growing up in Korea and the United States. The first book is about the year before my family moved to the United States. It's about a little girl and trying to hold onto all her fragmented memories of her homeland.

JUMP ROPE (an excerpt)

The last thing I remembered was my foot slipping and the unforgiving concrete steps scraping me as I tumbled to the echo of my own voice counting. Now, I lay still on the ground, my eyes closed shut tightly, afraid that if I opened them, all my bones would crumble like a cookie into dust. I laid there for a long time as I tried to quiet my breath, listening to the world going by, feeling the ant world crawling all around. I felt that if I moved, something terrible would happen to me.

That's when I heard the hysterical screams.

"My poor little puppy, my poor little puppy," she kept saying over and over again. I never understood why "puppy" was a term of endearment for Korean children, but it is as deeply ingrained in the language as a bowl of rice.

I felt her rushing over to me fussing like a mother. I kept still with my eyes closed, concentrating on keeping my bones together.

"Don't move me," I thought silently to her. "My bones will break. My body will fall apart and blow away into dust." My mom didn't listen.

She picked me up and held me to her bosom, still muttering, "my poor little puppy" the whole time. She patted my cheeks slightly and I finally opened my eyes, knowing that this little action would stop her small slaps.

"Are you OK? Do you feel anything broken?"

I shook my head. Negative. I hated being fussed over. I struggled to free myself from her maternal embrace and got up on my feet, dusting myself off. A crowd of kids had already gathered around us. I tried to ignore them and began examining myself. There were little abrasions all over my arms and legs, and I began to pick little pieces of gravel from the scuffs.

"Don't do that!" My mom yelled. Turning to my sister, she commanded, "Watch your sister while I go get some medicine."

Even before her familiar shape disappeared into the house, I turned my concentration back to separating the little stones from my bloody cuts. My sister muttered, "Mom said not to do that," half-heartedly as she went back to playing with her friends. A few of the younger kids, including my little brother, just stood there staring at me, as if they'd never seen anyone fall off a roof before.

We've all got stories to tell and a need to report them—
Let your stories out!

Writing

Get your favorite pen and some paper or a journal. It's your turn to write. We're going to make you a WriteGirl (or WriteGuy!)

Writing is about opening yourself to yourself. Your stories are already formed, they're just waiting for you to write them out. But they're a bit like rare birds—they hide when you go looking for them, so you have to build an environment where they'll come looking for you.

In this chapter, we will give you a few experiments (We call them "experiments" because "exercises" sound too much like work!) and some direction to help you cultivate the stillness, sensory perception, sense of adventure and climate of "yes" that you need in order to let loose your creative voice and reveal your own unique ideas, images and stories.

For each experiment, we'll give you specific creative writing techniques, followed by examples from WriteGirls to inspire and challenge you. You make the rules. Set a time limit or take as long as you want. Try writing in a cozy chair or in the sun. Have fun, and keep an open mind to whatever flows from your pen.

Experiments

Superhero/heroine Experiment

You are a superhero. What are your powers and what would you use them for? Give us all the details, from your name to your convictions. Use elements from your own life and play with them. Don't worry about starting from the beginning, just start writing what comes to you first. Just write. You can edit your work later.

Here is some space so you can start your experiment now!

Ariel Edwards-Levy, age 15

MY SECRET

Over the years, I have discovered something about myself. If anyone else tells me something confidential, my lips are sealed, but if the secret pertains only to me, it will escape my mouth in seconds flat.

So, after months of painful denial, I suppose that it's time for me to reveal my secret. I have superpowers. Believe me or not, as you wish. I say this only to uphold my integrity and cast light on truth, as well as because I need journalism credit.

I am fantastic. My powers are beyond your imagination. If only my outfits were skintight, Hollywood would make a movie about me, and populate the 99 Cent Stores with crappy action figures that bear no resemblance to me at all.

So, I hear you ask, why haven't you heard of me? Where are the headlines proclaiming daring rescues, exciting captures?

One word: school. And another: homework. Perhaps a third: apathy, actually. That pretty much sums it up.

The Anita Blake series by Laurell K. Hamilton inspired this piece. I discovered that I can use someone else's ideas and still be creative!

RITSUKO'S LIFE

I'm no ordinary girl. I'm magic! My name is Ritsuko and I have a special ability. Well, most humans think of it more as a disease. I consider it just another part of my life. I'm a lycanthrope. A lycanthrope is more commonly known as a wereanimal. Once a month, during the full moon, a human will shift into whatever type of lycanthrope infected them. The most well-known lycanthropes are the werewolves, but there are many types, such as wereleopards, wererats and werehyenas.

I, myself, am a wereleopard. During the full moon, I will shift into a leopard and roam the woods with my pard, or local, wereleopards to keep any rogue preternaturals away from vulnerable humans. When a preternatural goes rogue, it gives all of us a bad name, though it is not their fault. Something in their mind snapped. It is just like a mentally insane human cannot be held responsible for murder.

The preternaturals humans put in the movies are usually rogue because that sells more tickets. These movies give us a negative image because humans now see us as a threat. Not just lycanthropes, but vampires, zombies, even goblins and faeries are misrepresented and therefore judged wrong.

My pard looks to me for support because I am their Nimar-ra, their leopard queen. I lead the pard with my boyfriend Jayson, who is the Nimar-raj, the leopard king. We have been extremely lucky lately. There have been no rogues in over a month. Currently, the only thing to watch out for is the Ulfric, or wolf king, of the local werewolf pack. His Lupa, the wolf queen, has left him and, boy, is he upset!

Theresa Mulligan, mentor

LORDRA

My name is Lordra and I have the power of transport. I can be anywhere in the world in a nanosecond. I also have the power to read minds, which keeps me one step ahead of my enemies. My hair is bright red and down to my waist. I wear a T-shirt, a tennis skirt and gym shoes in the summer and flannel pajamas and slippers in the winter. Comfort is the name of the game when fighting off evil villains. I live in a loft apartment in Chicago. When it gets too cold, I transport to the Bahamas or Hawaii for the day. I know Kung Fu, Tae Kwon Do and Maga. I only get five times a year when I can become invisible. So, I use them wisely.

Portia Frazier, age 14

LAURA, EARTHMOVER

I am Terra Orchid, and I am an earthmover. The line between black and white for me turns gray. I have committed horrible crimes, and have no regrets, but I have saved the lives of entire cities. Unknown to those around me, I hide under the cover of a false name. I have a false life as well. To others, I am known as Laura Hilliard, a mild kindergarten teacher.

Erica Drennan, age 16

I decided to write from the perspective of Superman's little sister. At first I couldn't decide if she would have any powers of her own, but by just jumping into the piece I learned a lot more about my character than I expected to.

SUPERGIRL

Greetings. I'm Viola Murlin, 15 years old with brown hair and brown eyes, about 5'3" tall—pretty much average in all respects. Well, except for one thing. I happen to be Superman's little sister.

I bet you're all thinking that a) there's no such thing as Superman, and b) even if there were, he wouldn't have a little sister. Well, either way you're wrong. Superman is real. And he does have a sister—me. Of course, there's a 15-year age gap between us, so it's not like he lives at home, but still, it's nice to have him as an older brother. I certainly don't get beaten up at school.

Well, actually, that's not quite accurate. Nobody at school knows that Superman is my brother. They wouldn't believe me if I told them. No, the reason why I don't get beaten up is because I have superpowers, too.

I didn't always know I had superpowers. My parents figured one superhuman in the family was quite enough, thank you very much. They weren't too interested in trying to cultivate a "save the world" attitude in their younger child. But one day when I was six, Clark, being the idiot he is 99% of the time (funny how none of the stories about my brother mention that side of him), decided it would be funny to push his little sister off our 43rd floor fire escape overlooking Madison Avenue. As he tried to explain to our irritated mother, he really had planned to save me before I whizzed past Mrs. Rocklin's living room on the 14th floor, but it turned out he didn't have to. By the 37th floor I had a handle on flying, and was angry enough to fly right back up and push him off the other side of the fire escape. Needless to say, Clark had quite a few bruises the next day.

Ever since then, Clark and I have had what one might call a healthy brother-sister relationship. I go out of my way to lock him in burning houses, and he shoves me out windows whenever he gets the chance. It's quite harmless, though, and it certainly adds a little excitement to my life whenever he visits.

Having Superman as a brother isn't really all that weird. I mean, we're pretty used to all the reporters and the tourists by now. And almost everything I hear people say about my brother is accurate. There is one point I'd like to clear up, though. If Superman is really a Man of Steel like everyone says, then how come he cries whenever he gets a hangnail? So here's my message to America: give up on Steel Man over there. He's old school. Why bother with him when you can have me? I'm here. I'll wait. And in the meantime, you can find me in New Zealand. My new passion is extreme sports. Without any safety precautions, of course. What would be the fun in that?

Found Objects Experiment

We are surrounded by papers and objects. Right now, you have a house, backpack, purse or wallet full of things you have picked up along the way, or saved for a variety of reasons. These found objects can be terrific springboards for writing. Pick something in your possession. Look it over carefully. Feel its texture in your hand. Smell it. Hold it up to the light. Then write about whatever it gets you thinking about. Sometimes this experiment can tap into memories, dreams and fears. Go there. Go where the object takes you.

Start your experiment now!

Kari Golden, age 18

I picked up a missing child flyer, and this is what came out.

HAVE YOU SEEN US?

The fence that surrounds my house makes a clashing noise, and footsteps can be heard plopping their way across the wet cement. I am laying on the couch desperately hoping it isn't my father. Ladee jumps to her feet, gnawing and scratching at the slit in the wall where the mail comes through. I get up, trying to quiet her, but the growling doesn't subside until there is another crashing of the fence, and the plopping footsteps can be heard distancing themselves from our house. I walk toward the door to see a white rectangular paper with two fuzzy faces on the front, nestled on the floor, and plastered with footprints. HAVE YOU SEEN US? So the paper says, with the distraught faces glaring into the empty spaces of my home. They are lost, stuck somewhere in time, trapped. They need my help. HAVE YOU SEEN US? The paper leaks of tragedy and silent cries dying to be heard. My eyes narrow closer on the pictures, and I want to yell at them, "Where are you?! I can help you!" But human intellect jumps in, and I realize that there's going to be more tomorrow, and the day after that, and the day after that and the day after that... HAVE YOU SEEN US?

Johana Perez, age 16

We each randomly chose something from a table full of magazines and papers. I picked up a sports magazine. We had a time limit for this experiment—it was a lot of fun!

SENTINELS PRIDE

What a hunk, all muscular, tough and brave, hairy but that's okay.

How I wish I could say that about our football team.

We are either

Tall or small

Fat or skinny

One thing is for sure_they are all stinky.

I hate the smell, all that dirty sweat, especially

when they say "UUUMMM BABE"

Mini-skirts aren't my thing.

I am all cold, goosebumps up to my knees.

It's brutal to cheer for a losing team,

Touchdown "YEAH!!!"

Tumble "NO"

"RUN! RUN! NUMBER 22 RUN!"

All cocky, smart, cute as me, with a humongous butt.

By the way, that's our star.

I live it and suffer every day,

Experience it every Friday,

But for some reason I just can't get enough.

Three years of my life dedicated to a team.

Oops, time's up! Gotta finish this poem.

That's

Belmont High School Football Team.

Laura Hurtado, age 15

I picked up a high school sports magazine, which led me to write about my love of sports. I realized just how important this once embarrassing, but now funny, memory about my first fencing competition was to me. I learned that even a random sports magazine can recall memories which can be great starters for stories.

FIRST TIME JITTERS

Sports have always been a part of my life. When I'm not playing on a team, I am playing with friends. I love the anticipation, excitement and adrenaline pumping through my blood. But I can also get very nervous and tense before a competition. I have one memory that stands out, my first fencing competition...

It was a sweltering summer's day in Sacramento. Outside, it was nice—kids, families and their dogs roamed, fencing bags being lugged behind. But as soon as we went inside the competition area, it become claustrophobic, with buzzers constantly going off as fencers got touchés against their opponents. I couldn't hear myself speak because it was so loud. I felt dizzy; the air was blistering hot from the warm weather and too many sweaty people were clustered around. As I watched some of the other fencers, I wanted to run and hide for fear that I would make a fool of myself. I found myself dreading the weight of my multiple-layered fencing outfit.

But then I fenced a girl, Mya, for practice and easily beat her. So I started to feel better and began to think, "I can do this!" But that all changed when we were broken up into our groups and I saw how good the other girls were! I was so nervous that I began shaking uncontrollably. I was dehydrated and needed to drink but I was shaking so hard that I couldn't hold onto my Gatorade or put it to my mouth, and ended up spilling it all over my brand new white knickers, staining them! My coach tried to calm me down as my Dad held my head still with one hand and poured the Gatorade into my mouth with the other.

The bouts seemed never-ending, but in reality each was not much more than a minute long. In the end, I came in last place but I was too tired by that point to care! All I wanted to do was sleep. Yet now, when I look back on it, I laugh at the whole incident.

When it comes to sports, you have the good memories and the bad memories, those of wins and those of losses and bruises and even broken bones. But sometimes bad memories over the years can become funny to us and become good memories. And now I'm not so nervous anymore!

At the Creative Nonfiction Workshop, we looked at some flyers. We were asked to write about what they reminded us of. I picked up a Starbucks flyer and remembered the first time I went to one.

COFFEEISH

The first time I went to Starbucks, I was with my brother and his girlfriend. They spent awhile convincing me that coffee was good. It smelled nice, but it also smelled coffeeish. Coffee admittedly smells nice. I just hate the flavor.

I took a sip of the Frappuccino and was overwhelmed. Too much coffee. I spotted the cream and sugar. I poured in the cream to drown the coffee. Still too much. Sugar... no. Half and half... nearly, wjust nearly... no. Still too coffeeish. My brother looked at me like I had lost it.

The next time I went, I still loved the smell, except the smell of lush coffee is deceptive. I discovered the Grande Cream Frappuccino. Near ecstasy. And I didn't have to use half and half. I'm sure there's a metaphor here, some great meaning-of-life thing—I just don't know what.

Four Senses Experiment

We rely so much on what we see to tell us what to think. Close your eyes for one minute and take in all the non-visual stimuli. Feel the way your breath moves through your body. Dive into a conversation you can barely overhear. Smell the layers of coffee or laundry or grass in the air. Trace your fingers along the surface of your hand or whatever you are holding. Now write a poem about the something you just experienced.

Start your experiment now!

Victoria Shao, age 17

My mentor Gerry and I did the Four Senses experiment after the Poetry Workshop. We sat still for one minute with our eyes closed and wrote down all we sensed. It was amazing!

SATURDAY AT STARBUCKS

The sweet taste of chocolate and cider
on my tongue
People taking orders
Customers conversing in Spanish,
"¿Cuantos cuestan los pasteles?"
Beans being ground, drinks made
Toddlers' high-pitched voices
Jazz playing: piano, sax, voice
The squeak of wet boots on the tile floor
The slap of a pastry bin closing
The aroma of roasted beans mingled with cigarette smoke
The whirr of a refrigerator
The front door's unoiled hinges
The chink of coins in a cash register
The restroom door closing with a thud
The ripping receipt
The gentle rhythm of my body as I take each slow breath
The sensory richness
Starbucks on Saturday afternoon.

I did the four senses experiment while I was sitting outdoors in my courtyard in Venice having tea at sunset. I closed my eyes for a minute and observed all the stimuli. I didn't think I could make a poem out of nothing going on, but then the poem came very quickly.

WIND CHIMES

The tinkle-tangle clang of wind chimes
Weaves in, out, past, above and through
The incessant, irritating motor-powered whir
Of the cop chopper
Circling above my head.

Ah... teatime in Venice, California.
The sun's gone down over the rusty, stuccoed walls of the duplex next door.
The buttery yellow of my chunky Italian-clay teacup
Fades in the absence of light.

An airplane. That copter again. A fire siren's wail.
The wind chimes rising above them all
Like the taste of my ginger and lemon tea—
The pungent flavors fighting to be noticed
Above the acrid chlorine of Venetian tap water.

O great wind,
I hear you rustling the tops of the ancient palms
Joyous, fresh, undeterred, pushy
Clanging those wind chimes,
Tolling your church bells,
Demanding that I acknowledge
Change, change is all.

I feel you chilling my skin
As I sit in my red Polartec bathrobe
Drinking lukewarm tea at sunset.

JOURNEY THROUGH A NEUROTIC MIND

The assignment: Close your eyes for one minute and take in all the non-visual stimuli.

Okay. I can do this. Piece of cake. Where's the clock? Cool. One minute starts... now! Breathe in, breathe out, breathe in, breathe out....

Did I turn off the stove?

That pine-scented candle gave me a headache.

Why was my meeting cancelled?

Hailey's birthday is on Tuesday.

That ticking clock is really annoying.

Must get facial soon.

Yes, I definitely turned off the stove.

Talk to tall, dark and handsome tomorrow.

Pink is a pretty color... so are red and yellow.

Okay, stop! Must concentrate on non-visual stimuli. Breathe in, breathe out, breathe in, breathe out. That's it. That's...

Hey, why does that ticking clock sound even louder?

Pepperoni or cheese for dinner?

Is Francisco's soccer game tonight?

Call manager, reschedule meeting.

I think my foot just fell asleep.

Was that my cell phone?

Definitely pepperoni and cheese.

Boy, one minute is a very long time!

Outside Experiment

The details are what draw us into a news article, a letter or even a conversation. Specific details can turn a flat description into a sparkling and compelling slice of life. We just need to train ourselves to notice all the small and large events that are unfolding right in front of us every moment. Take yourself outside, anywhere outside. Take in everything you see. Try slowly sweeping your eyes from low to high, or from right to left. Take your time. Explore the colors, textures, shapes and contrasts. Take a full inventory of all your senses. Now write about what you see or how you feel.

Start your experiment now!

Laura Hurtado, age 15

I wrote this during the outdoor journalism exercise. Even though a day or a place may seem boring, sitting back and observing with all of your senses can really be inspiring!

OBSERVATIONS ON A RAINY DAY

Across the street, a man in his 40s walks his shaggy dog. He wears a red hat, a green jacket and slacks. He passes out of my range of sight. There seems to be nothing on this cold, dreary and drizzly day. Unless, of course, you are very quiet and are sure to use your senses. Then the scene suddenly comes alive. The sounds of cars on the next street over come into tune, splashing though the puddles of the earlier morning's rain; a crisp breeze flows through the air, chilling my bare arms and rustling the tree leaves like a cat batting its paw at a plaything. One by one, automobiles begin to drive by. First it's a white car and then a black SUV. Then it's an old beat up yellow van with a round window in the back. Next comes the parade of people: a woman dressed all in black strolls by, her head downward, causing the wisps of her hair that have escaped from her black beanie to blow across her cheeks, puffing away at her cigarette. An elderly man with glasses and a trench coat hurriedly goes by with an anti-war protest sign tucked under one arm. Following him, there's a family consisting of a mother, a father, a little girl and a little boy. Every few steps, one of them turns to look at me, curious. Finally, along comes an African-American man with long hair, singing a song, "...with every action, there is a reaction! Oh boy, oh boy... I'm so happy inside all the time..." I stifle a giggle. In one hand he carries a boom box that's turned off. In the other hand he holds a bag of dry-cleaning, which he has slung over his shoulder. I wonder what his story is. After he passes, the street lapses into quiet again until the protest march from a few blocks up ends and suddenly there is a whole swarm of people. It's time to go back inside, but just before I go through the door into the warmth, I turn back for one last look and notice the numerous raindrops on the asphalt and fence and benches, which I had overlooked before.

Sam Harris, age 17

THE STREET

There were cars parked up and down the street. Every few minutes, a lone vehicle would pass by. Several people were walking their dogs. The writers stood there, gazing into the street. Some pens moved rapidly, some only wiggled a little, then lay still. Several dozen eyes stared at the nearly empty road still wet from the morning rain. A family walked by, staring at the odd sight of thirty-some-odd girls and women watching the world around them. A man came by and began singing, pulling several giggles from the crowd. An old man asked where the boys were, getting even more laughter from the group. Two women stopped and stared as the old man explained what was happening. When told to return to the warmth of the inside, a few groans of protest drifted through the air, but WriteGirls obeyed.

Gaby Cardenas, age 16

It was a beautiful, cold day, so I wrote about how quiet it was.

TO GRATIFY SILENCE

Grey clouds today

Solemnly dispersed

It's been raining on and off

This is a gift

Blue and grey and ground and wet

Gratify it

It's cold outside

It's cold where I stand

It isn't pleasing

Being dry people

Being dry creatures by nature

It's hard to gratify

Such a contrast to our insides

And being out here

Here with the gentle caress

Of the wind's cold fingers

We shiver

We're not used to the touch and feel

Of silent detached kindness

Silence

We reflect this today

No living thing would

No less could

Make a sound

The tires on a car

Scraping on pavement

The soles of our shoes

Scraping on the asphalt

This is our only connection

Tying us together

Keeping us from floating off

When time is at a standstill

Heartbreaker Experiment

Tell us about someone who broke your heart. Give us all the details. Make a list of the qualities and personality traits of this heartbreaker that you remember. There's nothing like a strong emotion for getting the pen moving. Does it all have to be true? Sometimes we prevent ourselves from writing what we think we remember because we fear distorting the truth. So release yourself from that constraint, and write what you are compelled to write.

Start your experiment now!

WHO BROKE MY HEART?

He's the kind of person who can look you in your eye and tell a lie, without cracking a smile. He's the kind of person who can seem so sweet but does stupid things that really piss you off, like write you a ten-page letter saying that he loves you but he really loves your best friend.

He's the sort of person who you can love so much, but you want him to leave at the same time.

He's the sort of person who touches your cheeks with his freezing hands when it's already cold outside.

He's the sort of person who makes up lies to entertain himself.

Michelle Lewis, mentor

At the Character & Dialogue Workshop, my mentee, Allie, and I each wrote long lists of things about the person who broke our heart. When we got together for our weekly writing session, we decided to put this character in an unpleasant situation... We weren't done with him yet.

LOST IN LAS VEGAS II

Wolf woke up with a start to frantically flashing lights and the machine gun exhaust pipe of a motorcycle passing by. His eyelids felt like they were stapled shut, as he slowly became aware of the fact that he was sitting up. The wall against his back still held some warmth of the desert sun, though, as his eyes adjusted, he realized it was almost dawn.

An initial inventory of his surroundings didn't quite add up. Apparently, the flashing lights that woke him were on a sign directly over his head: "Chapel of Everlasting Love—Credit cards accepted."

"Oh, no," he muttered.

He stared down at the pavement and tried to force his brain to work extra hard, revving it like a car that just... won't... start.

Flashes of still-lifes appeared on the sidewalk like a slideshow: playing "Everything Falls Apart" at the Hard Rock, putting Frazier's cell number in his phone, a woman's face—dark lashes, Israeli-looking and scowling—just his type, the inside of a limo, the bathroom of a strip club, the woman's face again (really close to his this time), numbers on a cocktail napkin, a camera flash, sweat on his palms, a kiss, a camera flash, the guys in the band laughing.

Wolf willed his stare away from the sidewalk and onto his hand—and there it was—a wedding ring.

"Oh, no," he said, a bit louder.

LOST IN LAS VEGAS

When you're the sort of person who admires pants for how many holes they have in them, you're not necessarily the type of person with loads of common sense. And if your friends ditched you while you were in the bathroom in the middle of Las Vegas, and you're only 15—not only are you lacking in the common sense department, you're totally screwed. Such was Tom. With only $4.15 to his name he would somehow, eventually, find a way out of this debacle. Eventually. If he could stop thinking about just how delicious a sausage and pepperoni pizza would be right now. If he could stop thinking about that for 15.8 seconds, he would totally find a way out of this twist.

He sat down on a bench outside a small, run-down casino and closed his eyes for a moment. Give or take three hours.

When Tom did wake up, he didn't quite remember where he was. And then it hit him. Have you ever seen a blonde, 15-year-old boy cry? You would have if you had been in Las Vegas on this day.

Perspective Experiment

Describe someone unusual that you know, in each of three ways: from your perspective, from a family member's perspective and from the perspective of a neighbor. Truly, you don't need any further instructions!

Start your experiment now!

We designed this to use as the opening writing experiment for our Screenwriting Workshop. It was a great way to jump right into the complexity of character development. Here are responses from our girls and their mentors.

From my perspective:	Good dresser, fancy talker, class act.
From a family member:	Arrogant, big mouth, waste of time.
A neighbor's description:	Knows how to party.

From my perspective:	The AP English teacher is a Welsh man.
From a family member:	He's a pseudo-English nerd who rambles on and on while his listeners nod and scowl, confused but agreeing to his abstract, incomprehensible assertions.
A neighbor's description:	It's because he went to Harvard.

From my perspective:	Snake is not what he seems—despite his crazy outward persona, he's actually very down to earth and has become an amazing and devoted dad. Oh, and a little crazy too.
From a family member:	If that weird Snake character is at Christmas dinner again, it should be a fine evening – he's a real kick in the pants.
A neighbor's description:	Who's that guy with the orange Mohawk that's always visiting them at the country club?

From my perspective:	She's a free spirit, not afraid of pushing her world beyond its limits.
From a family member:	Young girls shouldn't wear black; it's just not right.
A neighbor's description:	Whatever happened to the little girl next door who used to come and have tea with me?

Three Steps to Happiness Experiment

Write how someone can make you happy in three steps. Be specific, like spelling out exactly what kind of chocolate you would want. It's surprising how focused you become in your writing when you have a limiting factor, like time, or as in this experiment, a finite number of statements you can use to make your case. And as any comedian knows, things are always funnier in groups of three.

Start your experiment now!

I wrote this during an audience exercise Keren led at the WriteGirl reading at Dutton's in Beverly Hills. I had just seen a PBS documentary on tango a couple of nights before, and it brought up such deep longing for Argentine tango (a music and dance that I adore). I hadn't danced tango in several years and realized that it was the perfect expression for a woman in midlife.

HOW TO MAKE ME HAPPY, IN THREE EASY STEPS

1. Be really, really hot. The hotter, the better. If you look like Antonio Banderas or Javier Bardem—GREAT!!!

2. Take ten tango lessons in a row, until the memory in your muscles holds every exquisite move and every subtle nuance perfectly.

3. Ask me to dance.

Wherever WriteGirls perform, we ask audience members to write with us. We pass out index cards, pens and provocative prompts to help everyone think, remember and create. Here are some responses from the audience at a reading at Dutton's Books in Beverly Hills.

1. Close the blinds but open the windows. Let the sounds in but not the light.
2. In the darkness of a cool L.A. breeze, feed me milk chocolate, in small bites.
3. Wrap me in wet seaweed and let me lay in my chocolate ocean of warmth for 40 days and nights.

1. You can stop me on the sidewalk to pet my dog.
2. You can tell me I look great – no matter how I look!
3. You can really pay attention to my answers, when you ask me a question like this!

1. Wake me gently.
2. Have coffee ready.
3. Let me watch football.

1. Write a sad poem about me.
2. Paint my poem on the bedroom wall.
3. Recite it to me every night before I fall asleep.

1. Rub my head.
2. Look in my eyes.
3. Listen to me for no more than 10 minutes.

1. Take me to Fuddrucker's.
2. Order me a delicious, brown half-pound original.
3. Watch me eat in silence.

1. Let me be unhappy.
2. Bake me a cake. Mix in words of quiet affirmation and loud laughter.
3. Help me to resist my fears.

1. When I say I'm right, don't disagree, even when I'm wrong.
2. Treat me to ice cream when I'm having a bad day.
3. Listen to me.

1. Tell the truth.
2. Make me laugh.
3. Always hope.

Identity Experiment

There are a few people who don't understand who you really are. Set them straight! Sometimes we need to lean into the very things we resist. This experiment takes you off the defensive position and gives you the opportunity to declare how you see yourself, right here, right now.

We asked passersby at our booth at the Los Angeles Times Festival of Books to take a moment to try this writing experiment. Even people who declare that they aren't writers, or that writing is too hard, manage to come up with something intriguing. Here's a sampling of their responses.

I am the culmination of all my life's loves, hates, fears, decisions, experiences, mistakes, triumphs, hopes and beliefs. I am not who you assume me to be, but I am a little bit what you see. Do not fear me and do not assume, but approach with an open mind, willing heart and love of life... and we will get along just fine.

I think there's always that strange dichotomy between who you think you are and who people think you are. I am independent, strong and like to do what I want. Don't judge me.

I am who I am. I will be the weirdest person and do whatever I want. Nothing you say can change the person that I really am. I like who I am and I'm going to stay that way.

Jerry Buss, the Lakers' owner, still doesn't know that I am the world's best sportscaster, and a woman, so he hasn't hired me yet. But I am the greatest.

I often think that I have to hide who I am from others. I don a mask, I don several masks, when I interact with others. But I've realized that it doesn't matter what people think of me. All that matters is what I think of myself. I'm going to be who I want to be. I am black, I am Nigerian, I am Hispanic. I am an Emily Dickinson fanatic. I love rock and Latin alternative music. There are many facets to me. I do not fit a stereotype. I won't be pigeonholed, placed into a category. I am many things. I am unique. I am me.

A lot of people think I'm so mean or that I don't care about anything. But I'm not like that. Although I'm a dark person, I understand a lot of things and I wish I wasn't judged like that.

I am really a musician who would spend her day – her whole day, all day – playing, practicing, composing, if this pesky job wouldn't get in the way!

I'm not white, nor am I trying to be. It seems that being something I'm not is the only way that any of you will listen to what I'm saying. But I'm still part of your team so listen up. I have ideas too. I'm majorly creative and love every moment of life. I cry a lot, at sad movies, joyous moments and stressful times. And I'm always there when you need someone to cry with you... I'm not super quiet, I have so much to say... if you would only listen.

I am crazy but calm. I am good and bad. I am weird and normal. I am not just one thing.

Start your experiment now!

There is someone you need to say something to. If you were to sit down and write them a letter right now, who would you write to, and what would you say? This experiment always generates some highly-charged responses. It really demonstrates how powerful the written word can be in helping clarify our thoughts, our emotions and our intentions.

It seems that there are a lot of people who have an unwritten letter in their hearts. After doing this WriteGirl experiment, their letters made it from their hearts onto this page.

Someone I would write to would be my mother – she walked out of my life when I was about five years old. I'm now 35 years old. The only thing I want her to answer is "what happened?" I'm afraid I'll never get an answer.

I would write to my crush, and tell him how I've liked him since 3rd grade.

My father. You haven't been there for me but, no matter what you do, you will always be my father. So I have to love you. I could tell you I love you if I saw you more often.

My son, did I never teach you to say please and thank you?

Dear Mich, you have been very mean in school and that is why I'm not inviting you to my birthday party. I can invite you if you get nicer. Your friend, Valentina.

To those who think they are powerless: So many believe they have to accept what those in power tell them, whether that power be religion or government. If that power is being abused, you have every right to speak up and out!

I would write to my estranged brother to try and mend our relationship. Unfortunately, I've tried to do this before and he was not receptive. Maybe persistence is the key?

I would write a letter to everyone and tell them to do whatever you can for anyone, all the time, always. Even if you don't know them, you know them, do whatever you can.

I'd write to my best friend. I'd let her know that I'm very happy that she's officially someone's girlfriend, but that I miss that she's not around that much anymore! And then I'd let her know I love her and will always be her best friend.

God. He has some explaining to do. Ha ha! I would also like to ask questions, lots of questions!! Always ask why and never settle for the first answer.

I would write to my friends in New York and tell them I'm sorry I left.

I would like to write to my mother. I wish you could be proud of my accomplishments. I wish you could recognize that I am an excellent mother and have the relationship with my daughter I would have liked to have had with you. Someday may you realize you missed who I really am.

I would write to my daughter, who I need to speak to, but who isn't listening right now. I would tell her to come home and quit running from being a grownup and taking on responsibilities. I would tell her I love her and want to talk with her.

I'd write an open letter to the world asking why they are so blind to the ridiculousness happening every day.

There is a boy in my English class. I would write him a letter about how much I value our friendship.

Start your experiment now!

This workshop had the best and most positive, open energy of all the workshops I've been to yet!

I met some great new friends
with loads of talent
and lots of heart.

150 perspectives.

WriteGirl is 150 girls and women.

This is

WriteGirl

And more stories than can be counted.

The power of positive women can change the world.

It's a rush to do something with cool women that will nurture the future of very cool girls.

These WriteGirls are going to change the way women are viewed!

Inspiration is so hard to come by.
SO nice to know I can always
find it at WriteGirl.

I wish there had been a "WriteGirl"
when I was a kid.

EXPLORE

Once a month, the Yucca Community Center in Hollywood, California, is abuzz with life as girls and women fill the large room for a full day of writing, laughing, learning and sharing. We *explore* different writing genres and themes: fiction, screenwriting, journalism, songwriting, family, culture, relationships. The professionals, the experts, the WriteGirls lead us into the world of stories, the dance of poetry, the depths of our journals. Between bites of pizza and cookies, our ideas flow from our pens onto the paper.

WriteGirls say ...

I really enjoyed it. It's fun to express yourself, with people your age.

I LOVED today's workshop. I learned a lot as an aspiring journalist.

I started out this day nervous and scared; now I'm happy and feel like I belong. It surprised me how polite and nice everyone is, and whoever brought the brownies I give you a million thank yous.

Today I learned that I have absolutely no sense of rhythm at all, but I am also in complete awe of all of the talented songwriters here!

I loved the luxury of a day way deep into poetry – the words flowed like a chocolate river.

I can't believe I was able to read my stuff out loud not only once but several times and the more I read the less nervous I became – something that's never happened before – yeah!

The words come to life and I feel enthused and reinvigorated and can't wait for the next workshop.

CONNECT — One-on-one Mentoring

WriteGirl pairs girls with accomplished female journalists, novelists, poets, editors, TV and film writers, songwriters and marketing executives. Somewhere in Los Angeles, in a coffee shop in the Valley, a corner table in Orange County, a girl and a woman sit and write quietly into their journals. One is a mentor, the other being mentored, but sometimes, it's hard to tell who is who. Over the sound of espresso makers, two females share themselves in their words, *connect* and discover the joys of each other's lives through their writing. It's only a matter of time before a fresh story or poem is invented over a mocha with extra whipped cream.

WriteGirls confide ...

> Through my mentee's example, I've learned to take constructive criticism more gracefully and surprised myself with how much knowledge I had to share. I feel I've learned as much from her as she has from me.

> I'm digging the girl power!!

> Thank you very much for WriteGirl. It's the best program I've ever been part of and you should all be quite proud of yourselves.

Writing is meant to be read. We publish an annual anthology to *share* our ideas, our histories and our dreams with as wide a community as we can reach. We showcase our work on our Website and newsletter. And we challenge each other to enter contests, attend writers' events and get published as often as we can!

WriteGirls reveal ...

> I wrote my first poem in about twenty years. Wow. Nothing but WriteGirl could've gotten me to do that.

> Every girl has a unique and poetic way of describing the world. Oh – and sometimes the mentor writing sounds girl-like and the mentee writing so adult.

TRANSFORM `Performances`

Between tall bookshelves, on sun-drenched outdoor stages, in café gardens, in darkened theaters at book festivals, shy girls and pensive women *transform* into captivating personalities as WriteGirls raise their voices and perform for audiences large and small. And each year, we present our newest book at a Gala Celebration in front of hundreds of friends, family and celebrity guests.

WriteGirls reflect ...

I loved seeing my mentee's scene on the stage. She was laughing so hard at her own words. I think she really felt like a writer for the first time.

I don't think that I'm ready for an audience of 10,000+, but I will use these new skills and soon be able to talk to anybody.

I look forward to reading and showing the world what I have to say.

It's so incredible to hear how witty and complex the minds of our WriteGirls are.

There is NOTHING, ABSOLUTELY NOTHING, not even a giant steel wall, that could keep me from experiencing WRITEGIRL next season, and the one after that, and the one after that, etc!

Leadership: The WriteGirl "Engine"

Executive Director	**Keren Taylor**
Associate Director	**Allison Deegan**
Administrative Manager	**Cecilia Lee**
Administrative Assistant	**Lori Obregon**
Website & Graphics	**Sara Apelkvist**
Publications	**Janine Coughlin, Karen Girard**
Book Sales	**Kathryn O'Brien**
Public Relations	**Shannon Johnson**
Membership	**Nanci Katz**
Curriculum & Guides	**Melinda Metz**
Mentoring	**Liliana Olivares Perez**
Workshops	**Kim Purcell**
Special Events	**Carlynne McDonnell, Retta Putignano**
Readings	**Caroline Siemers**

WriteGirl Advisory Board

Barbara Abercrombie, Novelist, UCLA Writing Instructor, Lecturer

Shelley Berger, Poet and Beyond Baroque Poetry Teacher

Mark Bisgeier, Entertainment Attorney

Suzie Coelho, Lifestyle Expert, Author, HGTV Television Host

Allison Deegan, Marketing Consultant, Screenwriter

Kai EL´ Zabar, Writer, Editor, Multimedia Consultant

Elizabeth Forsythe Hailey, Novelist

Mollie Gregory, Author, Teacher, Consultant for Writers

John Marshall, Vice President-Manufacturing, RR Donnelley

Vickie Nam, Writer, Editor of *Yell-Oh Girls* (Asian-American teen anthology), Interactive
Producer

Maria del Pilar O'Cadiz, Ph.D., Executive Director and Research Specialist/
Collaborative After School Project, California Department of Education

Joy Picus, Former L.A. Councilwoman, Community Organizer

Cecilia Rasmussen, Writer and Columnist for the *Los Angeles Times*

Debbie Reber, Author

Aleida Rodríguez, Poet, Editor, Educator, Translator, Publisher

Diane Siegel, Museum Educator, Community Organizer, Teacher, Los Angeles Public
Library Consultant

Keren Taylor, Songwriter, Poet, Visual Artist (Founder and WriteGirl Executive Director)

Participating Schools

Apple Valley Middle School

Belmont High School

Calabasas High School

Centennial High School

Claremont High School

Crescenta Valley High School

Crossroads School

Eagle Rock High School

Fairfax High School

Hamilton High School

Harvard-Westlake School

High Tech High School

Immaculate Heart Middle and High Schools

John Burroughs Middle School

John Marshall High School

Jordan High School

Marlborough School

Metropolitan High School

North Hollywood High School

Pacific Hills School

Pacific Ridge School

Palisades Charter High School

Redlands High School

Renaissance Academy

San Pedro High School

St. Margaret's Episcopal School

St. Paul High School

Torrance High School

Van Nuys High School

Referring Organizations

Bresee Community Center

Los Angeles Mentoring Coalition

Los Angeles Times

Para Los Ninos

Poets & Writers Magazine

UCLA Extension Writers Program

VolunteerMatch

Writers Guild of America, West

Writers Guild of America Foundation

Yucca Community Center

WriteGirl Supporters

WriteGirl would like to thank the following for their generous support:

Foundations and Corporations:

Ahmanson Foundation

Annenberg Foundation

Eli & Edythe L. Broad Foundation

Cal National Bank

City of Los Angeles Cultural Affairs Department, Youth Arts and Education Program

Los Angeles Unified School District – Beyond the Bell Branch

Oder Family Foundation

Roth Family Foundation

RR Donnelley

Writers Guild of America

Writers Guild of America Foundation

Union Bank of California

Individuals (a partial list)

Anonymous

Stephanie Allen

Barbara & Jon Avnet

Amy Berg

Janie Chavers

Jeff Criswell

Barbara Corday

Ann Daniel

Suzanne Dunaway

Sonya Elena

Michael Fister

David & Joan Gale

Sarah Goldfinger

Hildy Gottlieb-Hill

Lois & Dixon Harwin

Karen Jantzen

Monica Karo

Deana E. Katz

Tammy Kaitz & Steve Crane

Alyson & Lawrence H. Krasner

Mary Leslie

Georgianne Levangie & Brian Grazer

Joel Leder

Pat Lee

Jason Linn

Chris Lynch

Susan Lyne

John and Sandy Marshall

Theresa Mulligan

Jan Nash

Lori and Frank Obregon

Cilda Shaur O'Donnell

Marcia Paonessy

Aimee Pitta

Lori A. Pitta

Vincent F. Pitta

Angela Rinaldi

Nancy Ritter

Marc Silverstein

Jill Sirulnick

Norine Spadaro

Michelle Steffes

Allison Thomas

Beegie Truesdale

Nia Vardalos

Lynn Wasserman

Julie Waxman

Joan Stein Weiant

Clarissa Weirick

John Wells

WriteGirl gratefully acknowledges the following individuals, companies and organizations for their generous contributions:

Advisory Board Members for support and guidance on strategy, fundraising, communications and development of community partnerships

All of WriteGirl's mentors and volunteers for professional services, including strategic planning, public relations, event coordination, mentoring management, training and curriculum development, catering, financial management and administrative assistance

Albertson's for water at our workshops

Amano Books, Avalanche Publishing, BrushDance Inc., Chronicle Books and K. Schweitzer for journals for all members

Christophe Salon for gift certificates

Councilman Eric Garcetti and Councilman Tom LaBonge (Los Angeles City Council) for acknowledgement of WriteGirl's contribution to the community

Daisy Rock Guitars for an acoustic guitar

eventures for event coordination

Fabric Interactive and Sara Apelkvist for design and branding strategy, including development of WriteGirl's logo, Website, press kit, stationery, publications and ongoing support

FedEx Kinko's for photocopying and discounted services

French 75 Bistro for catering services

Los Angeles Times **Festival of Books and West Hollywood Book Fair** for donating WriteGirl booth space and promotional support at these events

Cecilia Lee for catering

Tim Maloney for audio visual and ongoing support

Jacques Taylor and BioConstructs (www.bioconstructs.com) for ongoing support

Trader Joe's for snacks and refreshments

UCLA Extension Writer's Program for assistance in recruiting mentors and volunteers for WriteGirl through its faculty and student populations

Writers Guild of America, West, and Writers Guild Foundation for publicity and support

Wright Graphics for printing of programs

Yucca Community Center for workshop and meeting space

Susan Abram is a reporter for the *Los Angeles Daily News,* where she covers county is-
sues. She has written stories for the *Los Angeles Times* and *LA Weekly,* and has worked
as a reporter in Connecticut and New York.

Melissa Anderson is a Los Angeles screenwriter and columnist, and is hoping to add
novelist to the list before her birthday this year.

Anna Artyushkina recently moved from Russia, where she graduated from the MUH
with a master's degree in linguistics. She was an English language and foreign literature
teacher, a freelance writer for entertainment magazines and a translator of foreign films.

Susan Benton has worked for global communications firms and has been published
online and in technical, healthcare and lifestyle publications, including *Electronic
News* and the *West End-Clayton Word.* She graduated from the University of Missouri
– St. Louis.

Jaime Buddle is a screenwriter and story editor in reality television. A recent script,
The Doubt Dragon, placed as a finalist in the 7th Annual Scriptapalooza screenwriting
competition. She has a master's in screenwriting from the American Film Institute.

Marna Bunger, working with Fortune 100 companies, government, nonprofits, small
businesses, startups and agencies, has more than 15 years of senior-level marketing and
communications success. She finds humor in her own life and beyond as the creative
force behind dontmincewords.com.

Elena Karina Byrne (*The Flammable Bird,* Zoo Press) is an artist, teacher, and curates
the reading series for USC's Doheny Memorial Library and The Ruskin Art Club. You will
find her in *Best American Poetry 2005* and at the ocean.

Silvia Cardenas is a TV/film writer. She's written on such shows as *Moesha, The
Brothers Garcia, The Proud Family, Raising Dad* and *Fatherhood.* Currently, she's writing her first feature for Paramount Studios.

Janine Coughlin is senior vice president of television series at Alliance Atlantis. She
writes essays and short stories, and is always looking for ways to marry her passion for
food and cooking with her writing.

M. Irene Daniel, aside from being an attorney and first-time novelist, is a Desert Rat.
Born and raised in a tiny rural community in central Arizona, she moved to Los Angeles
to attend law school at UCLA. She now resides with her husband and two cats in Eagle
Rock, California.

Leslie Davis is managing editor of *Nurses World Magazine,* a lifestyle publication for
California nurses. She was previously executive editor of Metro Magazine and dabbled

in environmental consulting. She graduated with a degree in print journalism from Boston's Emerson College.

Allison Deegan is a screenwriter and marketing consultant. She is WriteGirl's associate director and serves on the Advisory Board.

Geraldine Farrell's latest project, DRUMMIN' UP PEACE, a one-act play on conflict resolution, is touring Southern California schools. Her award-winning one-woman show, BEATRICE, has been seen on stage and heard on radio throughout the United States and Canada.

Katherine Fleming contributes monthly to *Allure* magazine. She is currently working on a sick and twisted illustrated gift book about friendship in addition to a feature-length screenplay. She will be directing her short film in summer 2005.

Hilary Galanoy is a feature-film screenwriter who has written projects for MGM, Paramount, Universal, Disney and New Regency. She's also a devotee of Ashtanga Yoga and a whiz at the barbecue.

Elizabeth Gill is a screenwriter who enjoys writing fiction and poetry. Her credits include television movies, as well as the series *My So-Called Life*. She teaches screenwriting at USC and UCLA Extension, and is the mother of two grown daughters.

Karen Girard, originally from the fierce woods of rural Massachusetts, is a poet and writer with a Ph.D. from Stanford. Her works include children's workbooks and educational booklets. She loves running and is currently working on her first novel.

Jessica Goldstein has written for the WB sitcoms *Family Affair* and *Run of the House* and UPN's *Cuts*. She also wrote for VH1 and wound up in a sketch with Nick Lachey. Her last line was "...you're really, really hot."

Nika Hoffman has taught creative writing, English and film for sixteen years. Her stories, poems and critical essays have appeared in a number of national publications. The high school journal she supervises has won many state and national awards.

Cara Haycak is a young adult author. Her first novel, *Red Palms* (Random House), was published in November 2004, and the second book is in the works.

Jennifer Hoppe has been a screenwriter since 1997. Her *The Dead Will Tell*, starring Anne Heche, aired on CBS in October. She has written scripts for Warner Brothers, DreamWorks, Columbia, HBO, Universal and Jersey, and is presently writing a feature for Paramount.

Lexa Houska is a copywriter for Frederick's of Hollywood. When she's not singing the praises of underpants, she writes children's stories, animation shorts and screenplays, and sings at the top of her lungs in the shower.

Shannon Johnson-Haber is the director of communications for the Los Angeles Unified School District, Facilities Services Division. She oversees all public relations strategies for the division's $14 billion new school construction and modernization program. Shannon also loves to write poetry.

Cara Jones is a singer and songwriter with credits on more than 40 albums, including three solo albums. Her songs have appeared in feature films and television internationally. She holds bachelor's and master's degrees from Harvard-Radcliffe and speaks Japanese. www.carajones.com

Nanci Katz is a screenwriter from Brooklyn, New York. She re-wrote a Lion's Gate Movie, *The Big Bang Theory;* adapted an ABC television movie, *Stickfigure;* and created a CBC radio documentary on romance writers. Oddest job? A singing-telegram gorilla.

Cecilia Hae-Jin Lee is a freelance writer, artist, photographer, poet and chef. Author of the cookbook *Eating Korean,* she writes food, art, culture and travel articles for anyone who'll pay her. She paints, eats and makes furniture in her spare time.

Michelle Lewis first wanted to write songs for other artists after discovering several had recorded songs from her albums. Currently, she's working with Fefe Dobson, Lillix and her own band, The Dilettantes. She is still homesick for her native NYC.

Amirah May Limayo recently graduated from California State University-Northridge's programs in English and Asian-American Studies. She hopes to teach creative writing while continuing to a master's degree. She loves to read and write stories relating to Asian-American literature.

Amy Morton is the assistant manager of editorial services at MGM Home Entertainment, where she writes and edits the text you see on DVDs such as *Hotel Rwanda.* Next up on her agenda: travel writing!

Theresa Mulligan is a television comedy writer. Her credits include *Greetings from Tucson, Run of the House, Method & Red* and *South Park.* She's originally from the Midwest and has a cat named Frank and a man named Jeff.

Kathryn O'Brien is currently in the process of writing her first mystery novel, which she plans to develop into an ongoing series. Past writing adventures include stage plays, spec film and TV scripts, film criticism and corporate communications.

Liliana Olivares-Perez, a Los Angeles native, earned her master's in screenwriting from the American Film Institute. Writer of the award-winning *Mi Piñata* and featured in *Latina* magazine, she is a WriteGirl four-year veteran and works for a reality-television production company.

Kristin Petersen grew up in Nebraska, but came to California to study at USC. She graduated in 2003 with degrees in journalism and economics. Currently, Kristin is a project manager at Guild Communications, a public affairs firm based in Washington, D.C.

Alix K. Pham is a screenwriter and poet. Her first screenplay, *Skin*, is being shopped around by producers. She is currently working on her second screenplay, *Forever*, an intense drama about co-dependence and alcoholism.

Anh Chi Pham is a graduate of Antioch University Los Angeles' M.F.A. Program and a former resident at Ragdale Foundation. Her first published story, *Mandala*, has been nominated for the 2005 Pushcart Prize. She is currently working on a novel.

Kimberly Purcell is a radio reporter turned novelist. She is currently doing a rewrite of her first novel, *Thicker than Water*, which is about a teenage girl who has been kidnapped by her biological father.

Marietta Putignano is currently editing her first novel, working on a screenplay and a one-act. This anthology will be her first print publication. In addition to being an actress, she is also a personal trainer and a painter. She is currently studying dancing and Italian.

Faryl Saliman Reingold's colorful career has ranged from entertainment journalism to production coordination for six Oscars' broadcasts. She recently earned a master's from USC and is writing a lifestyle manual to help people with spinal-cord injuries avoid pressure sores.

Jennifer Repo is a literary agent with Joelle Delbourgo Associates. A former editor with the Penguin Group, she worked on such books as, *The Art of Happiness*, *What's Next?* and *Eat Right 4 Your Type*. She is always searching for talented writers!

Mae Respicio is completing her first novel through fellowships from PEN Center USA and the Atlantic Center for the Arts. She first wrote in her journal at age six because her mom made her do it.

Diana Rico is an author *(Kovacsland: A Biography of Ernie Kovacs)*, TV producer/writer (18 *E! True Hollywood Stories*) and arts journalist. She has received two fellowships to write her passion project, a feature screenplay about Cuban artist Ana Mendieta.

Jayna Rust is an eighth grade language arts teacher and Teach For America corps member. She graduated from MU's School of Journalism while working as a sports reporter. She is now beginning her return to journalism.

Fabiola Sandoval is a community activist/mama/writer who is a member of the Downtown Women's Action Coalition and volunteers for the Los Angeles Community Action Network. She's creating a zine, contributes to a local paper and reads for pleasure.

Christiane Schull is a ghostwriter, screenwriter, breathwork practitioner and documentary filmmaker. She is at work on a film and book about tragedy and redemption involving 2,000 French-Canadian survivors who as children were interned in asylums.

Colleen Sharkey is a science writer and public-outreach coordinator for NASA's Jet Propulsion Laboratory. She graduated from the University of Cincinnati with a B.A. in English literature and is currently writing a master's thesis on the spoof newspaper, *The Onion.*

Jill Sheffield is a graduate of Sarah Lawrence College and recently received an M.F.A. in writing for children and young adults from Vermont College. She has been a copywriter for many years and writes funny, magical realism young adult novels.

Claire Bidwell Smith is the volunteer coordinator for 826LA, a nonprofit tutoring organization in Venice Beach. She holds a B.A. in creative writing from The New School for Social Research and is currently working on her first book.

Shauna Smith lives in Hollywood and works in the natural foods industry. She writes poetry and bits and pieces of creative nonfiction. She has been involved with WriteGirl for two years and is loving it!

Shelley Pannill Stein is a freelance journalist who has written for major daily newspapers, wires and national magazines, including *Forbes, ASAP, Worth, AFP* and the *Newark Star-Ledger.* She has also taught French to tenth graders in New York City.

Amaree Tanawong is a mergers and acquisitions tax consultant at Ernst and Young. She graduated from Emory University with a B.A. in French and English Literature. She hopes to one day quit her job and return to Paris!

Katherine Taylor earned her M.F.A. at Columbia University, where she was a Graduate Writing Fellow. She has won a Pushcart Prize and a McGinnis-Ritchie Award for Fiction. Her first novel and collection of stories are forthcoming from HarperCollins.

When **Dana Valenzuela** isn't writing a press release, a media alert or a corporate biography for one of her clients, she's dreaming of someday writing something longer than three pages. She hopes it might bring a few laughs.

Melissa Carolus Verlet has worked in journalism and education. She teaches history at the Archer School for Girls in Brentwood. She was a 2002–2003 Fulbright Fellow in France and is finishing her dissertation in European History at UCLA.

Marlys West's book of poems, *Notes for a Late-Blooming Martyr,* was published by the University of Akron Press in 1999. She was a Hodder Fellow at Princeton University and received an NEA grant for poetry.

Stacy N. Williams is a third-year English teacher and journalism advisor at Banning High School in Wilmington. She is also working toward her master's degree in professional writing with a concentration in creative nonfiction at USC.

Index by Author

About the Editor

Keren Taylor is the founder and Executive Director of WriteGirl. Passionate about inspiring others to cultivate their creative ideas, Keren has conducted hundreds of creative writing workshops for both youth and adults in Los Angeles and New York City. She has also led staff development workshops on literacy programming for the California Department of Education, LA's BEST, the YWCA, the New York Partnership for After-school Education and the Children's Creative Writing Campaign. Keren has performed her original music across the country in concert halls, theatres, clubs and festivals with her a cappella vocal group, The Trembles, and as a solo artist. She has opened for such acts as Blood, Sweat & Tears, Marvin Hamlisch, Dana Carvey, Frank Sinatra Junior and Gladys Knight. Keren spent a year in Las Vegas as a featured act at the New York New York Hotel & Casino. Her poetry appears in many literary journals as well as *So Luminous the Wildflowers – An Anthology of California Poetry* from Tebot Bach Press.

From Vancouver, Canada, she now lives in Los Angeles with her husband, Jacques Henri Taylor, and their chocolate lab, Wasabi.

About WriteGirl

WriteGirl is a creative writing and mentoring program that pairs professional women writers with teen girls. Through one-on-one mentoring, monthly workshops, public readings and publications, WriteGirl gives girls techniques, insights and hot tips for great writing in all genres. WriteGirls support, encourage and challenge each other to express themselves and their ideas and dreams, on paper and out loud. The result is a channeling of thoughts and emotions, improved self-confidence and life skills and, most importantly, a window to a wide world of possibilities.

WriteGirl, a project of nonprofit organization Community Partners, was founded in December 2001 in Los Angeles.

Other publications by WriteGirl

Threads, 2002
Bold Ink: Collected Voices of Women & Girls, 2003
Pieces of Me: The Voices of WriteGirl, 2004

WriteGirl welcomes your support: Visit WriteGirl on the web at **www.writegirl.org**